RETIREMENT PLANNING IN 8 STEPS

Quick-Start Guide

JOEL KRANC

RETIREMENT PLANNING IN

STEPS

THE PRACTICAL GUIDE TO SECURING YOUR FINANCIAL WELLBEING

TYCHO
PRESS

Contents

Introduction

Most people make two big mistakes when they think about saving for retirement.

First, they tend to think of retirement as an end goal, when nothing could be further from the truth. Planning your retirement does not end when you turn 65 years old. It should be part of the savings and income strategy you carry throughout your life before and after retirement.

Second, people assume that after a certain age, there is no point in trying to save money anymore. Actually, it's never too late to start planning for retirement. Sure, if you save early and consistently, you will enjoy a more secure retirement with a lifestyle that's comfortable for you. However, regardless of age and income level, it is always a good idea to prepare, save, and invest for your retirement years. The types of investments you choose as you age may be different than those of a younger investor, and there may be some catching up to do, but it is never too late to invest in your future. If you haven't already started, now is the time to begin.

Why now? Why has retirement planning become such an important part of our income-acquiring strategy in the 21st century?

America today is a very different place than it was post–World War II. Employees are very mobile, often changing jobs three or four times over their lifetimes. In the post–World War II era, people often worked at the same job or company for their entire careers with the promise of a secure pension once they retired. That pension, more technically known as a **defined benefit (DB)** pension plan, was the monetary promise given for years of service by your employer. Money you contributed to the plan, along with your employer's contributions, was managed by the company, and a work/age/salary formula often determined the amount you received in your pension check.

Over time, the cost of operating DB plans became very expensive, especially in down-market cycles, so employers began offering **defined contribution (DC)** or 401(k) plans. DC plans are a more cost-effective retirement solution for the employer but with more burdens on the employee. Employees are asked to contribute more money, select where they would like their money invested, and act as their own investment managers, which is not something many people are capable of doing.

Those factors, combined with the fact that we live much longer than people in previous generations, have made the need for secure and prudent retirement planning even more important.

This book offers eight steps to help get you on the path to a retirement plan that makes sense for you. You can certainly follow the book step-by-step, but keep in mind that many steps will overlap and that financial planning is an evolving process.

Within the steps, you will find strategies to help you reach your financial goals and achieve your desired lifestyle, regardless of your income and savings up until this point. You'll become educated about different types of investments and how they can fit within your plan. I have also included worksheets you can fill out to help you stay on track.

When you learn the right strategies, investing and navigating the markets will become much less over whelming. So let's get started today.

ASSESS YOUR NEEDS

Envision Your Ideal Retirement

The idea of retirement can sound romantic. Whether it's the images in the media or our own fantasies about what an "ideal" retirement looks like, we generally see a point in our lives where time is our own, responsibilities and obligations have waned, and we have endless possibilities.

When we reach retirement age, there are certain financial obligations that are usually part of the equation. Perhaps you have paid off your mortgage, your kids have finished school and are married, and most of your larger expenses are under control. Although some people are fortunate to have these items ticked off their list of obligations, other people struggle with expenses into their retirement years for a variety of reasons.

An ideal retirement will look different for everyone, despite what you've seen in the media. As you consider how best to prepare for retirement (financially or otherwise), be honest about what an ideal retirement looks like for you and not your neighbor or best friend.

Many workers today are staying at their jobs well into their retirement years, so you may envision yourself working longer or working in a consulting capacity. Or, you may be looking for the freedom to volunteer, travel, and do the things you didn't have time for when you were working full time. You may be forced to deal with **debt** and expenses and envision a retirement that looks much like your earlier working years. As you begin your retirement-planning journey, write down your dreams, plans, and obligations and realistically assess what is feasible and what is not.

According to a 2013 article in *Time* magazine titled "Redefining the 'Ideal' Retirement," there are several things you will want to consider when envisioning your own ideal, secure retirement.

- **Good health:** You can't predict your future health, but taking care of yourself will prepare you for a life of leisure. Staying active and healthy is as important as staying financially healthy, if not more. A structured workout regimen and proper diet can help ensure your retirement lasts a long time.

- **Finding a sense of purpose:** The leisure time of retirement usually takes place at the beginning of your retirement years. Traveling, playing golf, and sleeping late are fun for a while, but eventually a new reality will set in. What will you do now? This means different things to different people, but finding a sense of purpose is important for a healthy retirement. Have fun and get in that extra golf game, but start thinking of a new plan to make your days fulfilling with a purpose in mind. It could be anything from volunteering and spending more time with your grandkids to going back to school.

- **Working or not working:** Maybe you can't imagine not working. Either it is engrained in your nature, or you will become bored without a place to do business or use your skills. You might see your dream as a continuation of working full time, as a consultant, or in a part-time capacity. Perhaps you want to work, but you are interested in a completely different career from the one you had previously. If this is the case, write your goals down so you can see what is feasible. You may no longer be looking to climb a corporate ladder, so you can work in an environment you love without the stress of having to earn a paycheck.

- **Financial lifestyle:** It's hard to get too far into retirement without financial freedom and the ability to maintain a lifestyle to which you are accustomed. As this book will discuss, the right planning will provide you with a monthly income or steady income to fulfill your other dreams. Preparation is important as you fully immerse yourself into retirement, but so is proper maintenance of your finances.

- **Philanthropy:** Part of the larger retirement puzzle often includes sharing your wealth while you are living out your own dreams. With financial stability, you may have the desire to give back to the community, charities, and those you feel you may have neglected during your working years. Many Baby Boomers are retiring younger and living longer, and they are interested in leaving legacies.

These are just a few examples of goals, dreams, and ideas you may want to consider as you plan your retirement. Everyone is different. Your reasons for a secure retirement will differ from others depending on your social and economic status, demographics, culture, and even upbringing.

Whatever your desired dreams and goals, it's important to write them down to assess how and if they can be fulfilled. This is an exercise that can be done at any age and at any time. In fact, this should be done well before retirement, so your planning can match your dreams. Writing down your dreams allows you to see what is feasible, determine what can be taken off or put on the list, and discover how you will achieve those dreams later in life.

Financial Planning: Accuracy and Honesty

Goals, dreams, and visions are important and should not be discounted when starting your journey into retirement. But they will be difficult to achieve, without an accurate and honest assessment of your financial needs.

Let's start with the facts: Only a slight majority of Americans are saving for retirement. According to the Employee Benefit Research Institute and Matthew Greenwald & Associates 2013 Retirement Confidence Survey, 58 percent of workers are saving for retirement, down only 1 percent from 2012. The real issue is the declining trend, which showed that, in 2009, 65 percent of workers said they were saving for retirement.

TABLE 1.1: YOUR RETIREMENT DREAMS				
Writing down your dreams and goals will help you match your dreams to financial reality.				
Dream	**How Do I Achieve It?**	**Is It Feasible?**	**Is It a Need or a Want?**	**How Much Will It Cost?**
Good health				
Finding a purpose				
Working or not working				
Financial lifestyle				
Philanthropy				

Another issue is that many Americans are not saving enough money. The same survey shows that 57 percent of workers report they and/or their spouse have saved less than $25,000 in total savings, not including their DB plans and houses. That number includes 28 percent who say they have saved less than $1,000.

Unfortunately, the trouble does not end there. Thirty-one percent of Americans say they have had to take money from their retirement savings to pay for expenses over the last 12 months. More than half (53 percent) have not completed a retirement calculator, which is a basic tool for assessing financial needs in retirement and the amount needed to save to meet financial goals.

What do these statistics tell us?

Most Americans need to save more money. However, before you can start a financial plan to save more money, you have to (1) be honest with yourself about your knowledge on financial planning; (2) be honest about your savings habits; (3) look at how much money you have in the bank; and (4) decide how you intend to move forward from where you are today. The following quotes from businessman and investing expert Warren Buffett speak to these four points:

1. **"Risk comes from not knowing what you're doing."** Look at what you are doing or not doing and understand the gaps in your knowledge. There is no shame in lacking financial-planning knowledge and skills, but you can do something about it. The first question you should ask yourself is, "Am I being honest about my own financial-planning knowledge?"

   A Library of Congress/**US Securities and Exchange Commission** study about financial literacy found that Americans

   > . . . lack[ed] even a rudimentary understanding of stock and bond prices, risk diversification, portfolio choice, and investment fees. Furthermore, people that got one question correct were not particularly likely to get others correct, and "do not know" responses were quite widespread.

   These results are somewhat alarming. Remember, no advisor, **financial planner**, human resources department, or local bank manager will take care of your savings more than you will.

   For years, experts have discussed a greater need for financial education to begin at the very earliest stages of schooling. Teaching people early might spare them disappointment later in life. It might also increase saving rates and lower debt. So far, this has not been happening to a great enough extent. Educating yourself is the first step on the journey to financial freedom, and being honest about your limitations will help you take that first step.

2. **"If you buy things you don't need, you will soon sell things you need."** Being honest with yourself has to do with your spending (or lack of saving) habits. As stated earlier, 57 percent of workers report they and/or their spouse have saved less than $25,000 total, including 28 percent who have saved less than $1,000 total. A survey from Bankrate in 2013 reported that 30 percent of Americans had more credit card debt than emergency savings. A survey conducted by Bankrate in 2015 found that 37 percent of Americans are saving no more than 5 percent of income and one in five people are saving nothing at all.

If you don't think the expensive latte and extra manicure are adding up every month, think again. It's time you got realistic with yourself about your spending habits. Take very meticulous stock of your spending habits—not just the big items, but the smaller, everyday expenses you might not have previously considered.

Look at your paycheck, the amount of money you take home, and what you spend. Realistically assess if you can maintain that lifestyle when you are working and also when you are not.

3. **"Don't save what is left after spending; spend what is left after saving."** Accuracy and honesty in financial planning has to do with what you actually have saved. You may have gotten through the pain of assessing your savings rate and debt, but do you know what you actually have in the bank toward retirement?

For example, if your credit card debt, student loans, car payments, or mortgage payments are higher than what you are saving, take that into account when you look at the balance on your bank account. You may also have a 401(k) or DB plan with your employer. Consider this as well as you start taking the first steps of assessing your net worth.

In many ways, this step is one of the most important ones along your journey. If you don't know what you have, how will you know what you will need and determine your starting point?

The **subprime mortgage** crisis in 2008–2009 is a great example to remember. Many Americans at high financial risk were given loans they had no business taking. This is obviously a failing of the lending institutions; however, the people taking the loans were not honest about their worth, ability to pay when rates increased, and how much money it would take from their general savings to continue making payments. What resulted was a massive default on loans as interest rates rose and housing prices declined. Americans simply were not aware of what they had and what they could afford.

The takeaway: Don't fall into that trap. Make sure you know what you have before you embark on any further financial-planning assessments.

4. **"Someone's sitting in the shade today because someone planted a tree a long time ago."** Honesty and accuracy in relation to financial planning has to do with your future—knowing where you would like to be compared to where you are today.

   You may be thinking of where you would like to be in terms of travel and leisure time. However, the question should really be, "Where do I want to be financially?" Are you honestly and accurately able to achieve your financial plan? If not, will you have to change course to make it happen?

   The problem with the future is that it can't be predicted. You could win the lottery and not have to worry. More realistically, you might inherit money, get laid off, have kids, or go through a divorce. These types of events will affect your financial plan.

   It's best to look at realistic scenarios and how you can make your financial plan and **budget** (if you have one) work within them. If you know student loans will be part of your debt for some time, you can address fixed and variable costs accordingly and make an honest plan going forward. If you expect to have a family, consider the costs of schools, nannies, diapers, and formula. These costs are fixed for a certain amount of time and decrease as families mature.

   Although you can't perfectly predict your future, you can make logical choices based on a good understanding of yourself and your future trajectory. Later in this book, you will learn how your investment choices should match your lifestyle, age, and needs. In the meantime, by doing a first assessment, other pieces of your financial plan will be easier to address.

   This is a good time to consider all your sources of income and if you will need to revisit them based on your future goals. Will a new job with an employer who pays better or offers a pension plan be necessary? According to the US Department of Labor, only 54 percent of all workers are earning retirement benefits at work.

Getting all of these elements in order first and taking a realistic look at your life, goals, spending habits, debt, savings, and future needs are priorities. Doing this will help you create a proper retirement plan that will be realistic and fluid enough as your needs and wants change over time.

Calculating Savings and Expenses

You've taken the first step. You now have a more realistic and accurate picture of your financial self and what you may need in terms of financial planning. Next is a slightly harder exercise. How can you properly calculate your savings and expenses when you reach retirement?

There is no simple answer to this question. You won't know your exact needs, health status, and the kinds of hobbies or extracurricular activities you will be engaged in years from now. However, you can make logical assumptions that will help you make a reasonable calculation of your financial needs.

An article from *The Wall Street Journal* titled "Retirement 101: How to Figure Out What You'll Need" gives some pointers on how best to answer the calculation question.

1. **Figure out how much income you'll need.** The general rule is that, in order to live comfortably in retirement, most people will need about the same annual income they earned during their working years. Of course, you may now have little or no mortgage, your child obligations have waned, and other expenses have lessened or dissipated. However, it is still best to look at your disposable income today to understand what your disposable income in retirement should look like.

2. **Figure out how much you will get from outside sources.** There are a couple of elements to consider. First, how much will you receive from **Social Security**? That is likely one of your main sources of outside income.

   The US Social Security Administration states that Social Security benefits represent about 38 percent of the income of people 65 years and older. Among elderly beneficiaries, 52 percent of married couples and 74 percent of unmarried people receive 50 percent or more of their income from Social Security. Among elderly beneficiaries, 22 percent of married couples and about 47 percent of unmarried people rely on Social Security for 90 percent or more of their income.

   Is this you? Will 90 percent of your income come from Social Security, or do you (will you) have other sources on which to rely?

Second, if you are lucky enough to have a pension plan from your employer, consider it within your calculations. Social Security and your employer pension plan, combined, will help give you a rough estimate of your income in your retirement years, and if there are gaps, you need to fill them.

3. **Figure out how much income you will need from investments.** The gaps to be filled mentioned in tip 2 (the ones between government and your employer income) come from you and your investments. The investments that best suit your needs have not yet been discussed in detail; however, investments should fill income gaps and bring your income back to the level you were accustomed to during employment.

   The Wall Street Journal article gives a simple example. If you earned $40,000 during your career and expect to receive $23,000 from Social Security, you will need $17,000 per year from outside investments to fill the gap.

   The types of investments you make will depend on factors such as when you start investing, your tolerance for risk versus return, and whether you are looking for replacement income or something more. There are investments to suit all tolerances, stages in life, needs, and wants. You just have to know what you are looking for. This will be discussed in more depth in step 2.

4. **Understand how long your investments will have to last.** According to data from the US Census Bureau, the average American man will live to 75 years and the average American woman will live to 80 years. However, *The Wall Street Journal* article says these numbers are completely useless when talking about how long your investments will have to last.

   Why? The numbers measure average life expectancy from birth, not from age 65. Also, not everyone meets the average. Some people die earlier, and some die later.

   Much more useful, says the article, are the cohort survivorship figures calculated by the US Department of Health and Human Services. Of those who make it to age 65 years old, 25 percent will go on to live to 90 years old. For women, 30 percent will go on to live to 90 years old. Of the women who live to 65 years old, 12 percent will live to 95 years old and about 3 percent will live to be 100 years old. The bottom line: You want to ensure you have enough of a financial cushion in your retirement and leave money behind to your heirs rather than outliving your money.

To save "enough" for your retirement, you must ensure you have enough to last for 10, 20, and possibly 30 years past the age of 65. The task gets harder as people live longer and medical advances continue to prolong life, which is why it is more important than ever to plan today with very long-term goals in mind.

5.   **See steps 1 through 4.** Having gone through the first four steps, you should have a better sense of what you need and how you need to calculate your financial needs into retirement. The question becomes what types of investments will take you to your goals and keep you at income levels that will sustain you the rest of your life.

6.   **Annuities are the easiest example.** Annuities allow the investor to purchase an insurance-based investment product that provides a guaranteed income for the rest of their lives. If you plan to retire at age 65 and will need an income of $10,000 extra per year from your investments for the next 30 years, how much will you need to save?

A 65-year-old man who wants an income of $10,000 a year for life could buy an **annuity** for $130,000. You might think you should save about 13 or 14 times the extra income you need. However, most annuities do not account for inflation, which could cut your purchasing power by half if not protected properly.

If you start with **bonds** or blue-chip stocks (or **mutual funds**), you might expect a portfolio such as this to earn an average return of inflation plus about 3 percent over the course of an economic cycle. Based on these numbers, you probably need to set aside about 20 times your required annual income by the time you retire. If you need your investments to provide you with $10,000 a year and last about 30 years, you would likely want to start with about $200,000. If you need your investments to generate $50,000 a year, you would likely have to start with an investment of $1 million.

The bad news is that we have seen low numbers on savings rates (e.g., housing), and the rates are continuing to decline. Starting to save now is important, and being realistic will only make your choices about saving better in the long run.

What about your expenses in retirement? How will you know your future expenses, even if you have a handle on your income and outside income sources?

There are a few essential questions you should answer in order to best assess your expenses during retirement. By following the book to this point, you have a sense of your income or what you think it might be after your retirement.

The asset management firm BlackRock has created a worksheet for profiling expenses and asks investors taking the journey to retirement to consider the following expense items:

- **Essential versus discretionary spending: Essential spending** is relatively easy to define. Housing, utilities, food, and clothing are basic essentials everyone can anticipate and budget for in their retirement years. Essentials are relatively fixed costs that do not vary too much from month to month.

  Discretionary spending is more fluid. For example, will you be traveling, going out more, or spending more money on your kids? Even this type of spending can be calculated to some degree if you plan out your trips or know how many you will take per year. If money is tight or your investments are lacking in a particular year, discretionary spending can be reduced or eliminated altogether.

- **One-time expenses:** During retirement you may find that one-time, large-ticket expenses appear to be unexpected, but you can plan for them. Paying for a child's wedding or the latter years of a child or even a grandchild's education may be part of your expenses. Still, with a buffer or cushion of savings added into your calculations, you can avoid significant adjustments to your other expenses and still help your family at the same time.

Itemizing and categorizing your expenses (fixed, ongoing, and one-time) can help you with your planning now and in the long run. Ask yourself the following questions as you start looking at costs realistically.

- How many years are left on my mortgage?
- Do I plan on moving or downsizing my primary residence, and would I like to own a second home as well?
- Will my health insurance and/or premiums change as a result of my age and my retirement?
- Do I have the necessary insurance needed for long-term healthcare, or should I be budgeting more for additional premiums?
- Will I be spending significant amounts of money on hobbies, travel, and entertainment once I retire?

According to BlackRock, expenses should be monitored and assessed before retirement and during retirement. Expenses change over time, and any retirement financial plan will need to be fluid enough to adjust to these changes.

TABLE 1.2: CALCULATING YOUR SAVINGS AND EXPENSES

Use this chart to calculate your savings and expenses right now, and what you anticipate a year before retirement, and during retirement. It is expected that your numbers are best guesses. This exercise will still help you plan for the future.

	CURRENTLY	YR BEFORE RETIREMENT	DURING RETIREMENT
INCOME			
Total Monthly Income			
EXPENSES			
TAXES (VARIABLE WITH INCOME)			
Federal / State / Local			
HOUSEHOLD			
Mortgage / Utilities / Taxes			
Other			
AUTOS & TRANSPORTATION			
Fuel / Repairs / Insurance			
Other			
LIVING			
Food / Clothing			
Other			
MEDICAL / HEALTH			
Insurance Policies			
Out-of-Pocket Expenses			
Other			
FAMILY CARE			
Child Care / Assistance			
Other			
DISCRETIONARY EXPENSES			
Dining / Entertainment / Travel			
Other			
Total Expense			
BALANCE			
Total Income			
Total Expenses	−	−	−
Balance	=	=	=

Changing Needs over Time

From the moment you begin thinking about your retirement plan and assess what your needs will be, things are going to change. This is true during your working years and into retirement as well. In order to be prepared, or as prepared as possible, now is a good time to consider the factors that could change your financial needs between now and retirement.

Let's start with economics—wages, inflation, and buying power. In the age of smartphones, texting, and e-mail, you probably haven't thought of the price of a stamp in a while. However, if you looked at the price of a stamp in 1970, which was six cents, and compared it to today's price, which is 49 cents, you would notice an astronomic jump of more than 700 percent. That's inflation.

The **Consumer Price Index**, according to the US Department of Labor's Bureau of Labor Statistics, is defined as "changes in the prices paid by urban consumers for a representative basket of goods and services."

Why is this important? The Consumer Price Index takes a representative basket of goods consumed by urban households (e.g., food, clothes, and utilities) and uses it as an economic indicator to measure inflation. So, if you have reached a pinnacle of your career and/or your salary is at a place where it will likely stay pretty close to its current level, as prices (and inflation) rise, your purchasing power diminishes.

This is an important point. Even if you do nothing different over the course of your life and your other expenses remain the same, your buying power can diminish as inflation rises. A good rule of thumb, when measuring factors that can change between now and retirement, is to account for an annual rise of inflation of between 2 and 3 percent. Historically, since 1913, the average rate of inflation has been just more than 3 percent per year.

Nationwide Retirement Solutions offers the following example to illustrate how inflation can affect your portfolio.

If your investments don't keep pace with the rate of inflation, you may lose purchasing power. The difference between your investments' total rate of return and the inflation rate is often called the real rate of return. Here's a simple example:

If you invested money at a 5% interest rate and inflation also rises by 5%, you'll effectively not have earned anything. However, if the inflation for the year is only 2%, you'll have made a profit of 3% on your investments. Conversely, if your investments are earning 5% and inflation is, say, 7%, you'll have lost 2%.

Keep in mind that investing involves market risk, including possible loss of the money you've invested. And there is no guarantee you will achieve your investment goals. This illustration is only an example. It is not meant to project the returns of any specific investment. If fees and expenses had been deducted, the returns would have been lower.

Another need to consider is the cost of raising children. Although this cost plateaus and then declines over time, it does represent a large part of your expenses during your best earning years.

According to the US Department of Agriculture's annual report "Expenditure on Children by Families," the average cost of raising a child in America up to the age of 18 is $245,340. How is this amount determined?

- Housing and transportation: $107,970

- Childcare and education: $44,400

- Food: $39,060

- Clothing and miscellaneous: $33,780

- Healthcare: $20,130

Comparatively, in 1960, the first year the report was released, a middle-income family could have expected to spend $25,230 (or $198,560 in 2013 dollars) to raise a child until the age of 18. Housing was then, and is now, the largest expense for raising kids. Also of note, between 1960 and now, healthcare expenses have doubled for total childrearing costs.

These numbers do not take into account if you decide to send your child to private school, camp, or other extracurricular activities. Needs change, but these costs represent good starting points you can use to begin part of your retirement plan.

The US Department of Agriculture provides a "Cost of Raising a Child Calculator" (see Resources, page 134).

In 2013, the average annual healthcare premiums for employer-sponsored health insurance were, according to a report by the Kaiser Family Foundation, Health Research & Educational Trust, $5,884 for single coverage and $16,351 for family coverage.

The report also showed that health insurance premiums have risen 196 percent since 1999, with worker contributions growing 182 percent. Wages, however, have grown only 50 percent since 1999.

Also, according to the latest retiree healthcare cost estimate from Fidelity's Benefits Consulting Services, couples who start their retirement at 65 years old in 2014 will need an average of $220,000 to cover their medical expenses throughout retirement.

Luckily, that figure has been relatively stable since 2013, down from $250,000 in 2010. However, for many people, healthcare is one of the largest expenses after they retire. The $220,000 does not include costs associated with nursing home care and applies only to retirees with traditional **Medicare** insurance coverage, which will be discussed later in the book.

The message: If you're lucky, your health will not deteriorate over the course of your lifetime in any catastrophic way. Healthcare costs are going up and are not being met by wage increases. Factor in these costs and know that you will spend more on medications and tests later in life.

Downsizing may have a positive impact on expenses and needs. As your kids go to college or get married, your housing needs may change, and you may want a smaller place to live. You won't need the big yard or extra bedrooms, so downsizing your accommodations could benefit your expense calculations in the future. If you are close to paying off your mortgage or have paid it off, this can become a goal to check off your list as you reach retirement. Only you know your ability to pay off the mortgage and if you will reach that goal when you get close to retirement. Plan accordingly and make it part of your financial plan as you factor in your changing needs.

Baby Boomers are often known as the **sandwich generation**. Many Baby Boomers are still caring for and/or raising children but also dealing with the needs and costs of caring for elderly parents. These needs will change over time and should be considered as a factor within the retirement plan. Home care, elder care, medical costs, and nursing facilities may become part of your budgeting needs. Medicare will help pay for some of these costs but not for items such as nursing facilities.

If retiring early is a goal or dream of yours, this also is a changing need. Retiring early may or may not be feasible depending on how you have planned and assessed your finances. Social Security is reduced for people wanting to withdraw early and will be discussed more in step 5. Retiring early also lessens your earning years and potential saving years, thereby increasing the amount you will need to save prior to retirement. For example, someone born after 1960 would reach full retirement at age 67. If he or she wants to make an early withdrawal at age 62, a $1,000 retirement benefit would be reduced to $700 per month—a 30 percent reduction. A $500 spouse's benefit would be reduced to $325—a 35 percent reduction.

Taking an early retirement is your choice but should be part of your retirement planning and your understanding of how your needs change over time.

The overall premise is that the needs and the costs associated with living are never stagnant. When you are young, expenses are high and saving is difficult. Later in life, things change and saving should be slightly easier. However, planning and saving as early as possible will help as your needs change and unpredictable situations arise.

Taking stock of your financial needs and realistically assessing what you have and what you think you will need to maintain your lifestyle is the key to getting started on your retirement-planning journey.

Once you make real assessments, you will be better equipped to make financial and investment choices that will maintain and grow your income during your retirement years. As you progress through the book, the choices that can shape your financial plan will be explained in detail, giving you the tools to help you achieve your goals.

BUILD AN INVESTMENT PLAN

The Challenges of Retirement Planning

The first step in this book asked you to envision your ideal retirement, your dreams, and how these ideals would fit realistically into a financial plan.

Now is the real challenge: actual retirement planning. Whether that means creating your own plan, working with an advisor, using the resources provided by your employer, or a combination of these strategies, planning is no easy task.

The biggest challenge in retirement planning may be getting the process started. A Deloitte Center for Financial Services survey conducted in 2012 noted that 58 percent of Americans did not have a formal retirement savings and income plan in place. The further people were from retirement, the more this gap rose—to 70 percent among those who didn't expect to leave the workforce for at least 15 years. Also, 93 percent of respondents at least 15 years away from retirement who did not have a formal retirement plan believed Social Security would not meet their retirement needs.

If they didn't have a plan and didn't think the government would help them in their retirement years, why didn't they start making a plan?

Deloitte identified five barriers facing many Americans that prevent them from taking a direct approach to setting retirement goals and putting in place the required plan and structure to secure a sound financial future. They include the following:

- **Conflicting priorities:** It's hard to argue with immediate priorities. Other financial obligations that must be met sooner rather than later (e.g., house, car, kids, and taxes) are always top priorities in people's minds. Many people find it difficult to balance a much longer-term need or financial goal with the immediate needs facing them every day.

- **A failure to communicate:** Financial institutions have not been successful at communicating with clients about their retirement-planning needs, especially via the workplace. Even when financial planning is communicated, retirement planning is not often integrated into the consumer's needs as part of a broader financial strategy.

- **A lack of product awareness:** Many Americans are not familiar with the retirement products and options available to them, which is another symptom of lack of communication.

- **Mistrust in financial institutions and intermediaries:** The financial services industry's reputation has taken a beating since the **Great Recession** of 2007–2009. Many individuals do not trust financial service providers and their intermediaries (advisors) to provide objective advice and products, nor do people believe financial service providers can deliver on their promises to serve individuals' retirement needs.

- **The do-it-myself mentality:** Professional help can sometimes be shunned by consumers who feel they don't need or don't want the help. Some of this thinking is a result of people's focus on immediate obligations and lack of long-term thinking in regard to retirement planning.

No one is saying these are illegitimate challenges and are easy to overcome. However, according to the Deloitte report:

Changing the mindset of consumers and retirement services providers and encouraging a more integrated discipline to retirement planning is probably a very important step that can be taken to resolve the retirement dilemma.

There are other challenges involved in retirement planning beyond our own self-imposed or financial service industry–created barriers. For example, preparing a plan will force us to look at the issues of age and health. For example, will we outlive our retirement savings? Can we keep pace with rising costs and inflation as mentioned in step 1? How do we react to market uncertainty? Are we prepared for tax increases, and is insurance necessary to protect our retirement income?

Getting Started

The rest of this book aims to diminish these challenges and provide you with strategies to get over your own investment fears. What is the first and best thing you can do for yourself, now that you've looked at your goals and identified the key challenges you face?

Start early.

That's it. It seems like a simple and common sense approach, but it is often the key ingredient missing from many Americans' retirement plans, if they have a plan. As stated in the introduction, you are never too old to start saving for retirement, and it is never too late to begin. That said, the earlier you start, the better off you'll be.

The simple part of this idea is that the longer you save and the earlier you start saving for retirement, the more money you will accumulate. Even if you put the money under your mattress for 30 or more years, doing it longer will help you acquire more wealth for your retirement.

Compounding

There is another more compelling reason to start early when it comes to retirement savings: **compounding**. According to Investopedia, the definition of compounding is the following:

> *The ability of an asset to generate earnings, which are then reinvested in order to generate their own earnings. In other words, compounding refers to generating earnings from previous earnings.*

In simpler terms, if you invest money today, it can grow at a more robust rate because it is continuously invested, as opposed to if you started investing later with more assets.

Some of the ways in which you can take advantage of compounding include the following:

- **Earn interest on interest.** When returns are reinvested, these earnings can also produce interest.

- **Dividends can be used to invest into additional stocks or mutual funds.** More shares of stock can increase your **dividend** payments.

The US Securities and Exchange Commission provides a compound interest calculator (see Resources, page 134).

Catching Up

The earlier you start saving, the better, because compounding will have more time to grow your investments and you will have less catching up to do later in life. The other key is to leave the money invested once it has been put away. Taking it out or "borrowing" it adversely affects the compounding interest, so try not to tamper with it too much.

While catching up is not an ideal retirement savings strategy and it should not be your first option, it is something you can try to do once you start planning your retirement at any age. One of the first things you have to do, which may sound simple, is to "get over it." Get over your frustrations or past mistakes and stop kicking yourself for not having saved or invested earlier. That's done, so move on.

EXAMPLE OF COMPOUNDING

There are two investors, Paul and John. They are the same age, earn the same amount of money, and have the same obligations and decisions about saving their money and/or spending it.

Paul decides to start saving and investing his money relatively early at age 25, and he puts away $200 per month toward his retirement account. He continues contributing $200 per month for his entire career up to age 65, a total of 41 years.

John decides his current obligations need his attention and decides to wait until age 35 to start saving for retirement. He thinks that by investing $400 per month into a retirement account (twice as much as Paul) for 31 years, up to age 65, he will catch up to Paul's level of savings and they would have saved the same amount at the beginning of their retirement. He figures he can catch up by contributing more. The assumption is made that both investors earn 7 percent returns compounded monthly. However, look at the results.

	Paul	**John**
Contributions	$200 per month starting at age 25	$400 per month starting at age 35
Total contributions at age 65	$98,400	$148,800
Retirement fund value at 65 with 7% monthly compounding	$565,391	$528,222
Earnings	$466,991	$379,422

Unfortunately for John, he never catches up to Paul. The longer you wait to save for retirement, the harder it is to catch up and the greater your contributions need to be.

Some of the catch-up strategies to consider if you start saving late are the following:

- Increase taxable savings by reducing expenses and/or increasing income.

- Take assets that produce little to no income and convert them into investment savings.

- Take advantage of **tax-deferred** savings plans from your employer and the government.

- Consider direct-ownership investments (e.g., real estate, owning your own business to avoid brokers who take commissions and reduce your potential revenue stream).

- Consider retiring on less money by stretching the savings you have, redefining your entire retirement plan such that your catch-up savings burden is reduced.

Working Later

Compounding and catching up help explain why starting early is one of the most important retirement strategies. They also help explain the third reason for starting early, which is to avoid working longer than you have to or want to. Some people will reach retirement age and want to continue to work at a full-time or part-time capacity, but other people will not. They will want to enjoy their free time and do other things after committing to their careers for their entire adult lives. Working later into the retirement years is an option they want to avoid.

A 2013 Wells Fargo survey found that 37 percent of Americans feel they will either work until they die or are too sick to work. Another 42 percent say paying bills and saving for retirement (combined) is not possible. Couple this with a fear of investing and a lack of planning, and you have a recipe for little or no retirement savings.

The strategy of starting to save early is extremely important. Talk with friends and colleagues about their plans, the brokers or advisors they recommend, and where they cut costs and make their investments. This should be the starting point for getting your savings on the right track.

Creating a Cushion

Morningstar, a stock, bond, and mutual fund rating and analysis company, defines stock market **volatility** this way:

> *Historical statistical volatility is a measure of how much the stock price fluctuated during a given time period. While historical volatility can be indicative of future volatility, it can also differ greatly from future volatility, depending on what was driving the price changes during the past period. Major expected news items are more important drivers of big moves in the stock price in the near future.*

If you read this definition carefully, you might have noticed a seemingly confusing or contradicting point. Part of the definition says, "While historical volatility can be *indicative* of future volatility, it can also *differ greatly* from future volatility."

What does this mean for you?

By investing in markets, you cannot predict when or how volatility will occur and to what levels (severe versus less-aggressive price swings). This is why time and starting your investment planning early are so important. By creating a larger investment cushion over a longer period of time, you help counter the effects of market volatility and fluctuations on your investments.

Consider the Great Recession of 2007–2009, which was referenced earlier. On average, investors in the market lost between 30 and 50 percent of their asset value.

Although participants within private sector DB plans might have been somewhat sheltered from the equity losses, investors within 401(k) plans took a very substantial loss. Individuals saw equity values within their 401(k) plans or **individual retirement accounts (IRAs)** (more will be discussed about IRAs in step 3) decline by $2.8 trillion. By 2013, stock markets recovered to prerecession levels, retirement savings recovered, and workers saw a six-year period of no return on their investments. Combine that with a low interest rate environment, and you can see how volatility affects investors.

10 BEST WAYS TO INCREASE SAVINGS AND REDUCE EXPENSES

A consistent retirement savings plan cannot be avoided if you want to ensure a secure retirement that meets your needs and goals. Given that you have expenses to pay and you also need to find ways to save money, it is best to try to do both at the same time. The following list outlines some helpful ways to start.

1. **Always pay yourself first.** Yes, you have bills, taxes, car payments, and mortgage payments. These cannot be avoided, but one of the best ways to save money is the "out of sight out of mind" method. If you set up an automatic savings account where money from your pay is deducted and saved immediately, without you ever seeing it, it is more likely you won't spend it and will have it later for a rainy day, your retirement, or both.

2. **It's the little things that add up.** Every morning before you head off to work, you stop at your local five-dollar, high-end coffee establishment. You might grab a bagel or a pastry, and before you've sat down at your desk for the morning and earned a dollar, you've spent ten dollars or more. Eating at home before you leave is healthier and also less expensive. Ten dollars a day over the course of a year can save you $2,400 a year ($10 × 20 days per month × 12 months). Putting that money into your retirement fund will have a significant impact when you factor compounding and interest/investment returns.

3. **Maximize employer and government options.** There are many structured ways to save money for your retirement with very little effort on your part. First, if your employer offers a tax-deferred savings plan such as a 401(k), a match for your contributions is usually provided (this will be discussed more in step 3). By setting aside a percentage of your paycheck for the plan, you will gain money by saving but also by taking extra funds provided to you by your employer. IRAs are also a government-created, tax-deferred retirement vehicle similar to 401(k)s that allow you to save relatively easily with your local financial institution.

4. **Talk to your spouse.** Many couples don't have "the talk." In this case, we are referring to a talk about finances and what retirement will or should look like. A 2014 poll by *Money* magazine found that 70 percent of couples argue about money more than they fight about household chores, snoring, or sex. Getting past the fighting means getting closer to your goals. A good plan that involves input, strategy, and buy-in from you both will allow you to save more consistently with a common goal in mind.

5. **Make a budget.** While you're talking to your spouse about savings, it's not a bad time to consider making a proper household budget. Categorize your needs and wants; look realistically at expenses; and find ways to save, redirect, and repurpose how your money is being used for everyday needs. A good budget can go a long way in rooting out wasteful spending and creating the discipline needed for continuous saving.

6. **Eliminate debt.** All of us have debt. Some of it is "good" (like a mortgage), and some of it is "bad" (like a credit card), but we are all paying for something that we had to borrow money to purchase. Whenever possible, eliminating debt will free up more cash for you to save and put into your retirement fund. For example, doubling up on mortgage payments, getting rid of a car you might not really need, and paying off loans will help you in the long term.

   Consolidating debt may help you lower payments into one easy-to-understand monthly payment, but this strategy can have pitfalls. Interest might actually work out to be higher in the long run under a consolidated plan, and consolidation services may charge you more than is necessary. Consolidation can be helpful in reducing your expenses and increasing your savings but should never be used as a cure-all for your debt problems.

7. **Purge.** Everyone has unwanted items or things they just don't use anymore. We hold on to things for emotional reasons or with the idea that they might be useful again, but we know they will stay in their boxes never seeing the light of day. It's a good exercise to purge because you can increase savings and reduce expenses by selling unwanted items. In addition to being therapeutic and reclaiming parts of your garage, the extra money will come in handy toward your savings. Donations can also garner tax receipts, which is another way of saving.

8. **Eat in.** As mentioned earlier, meals out of the house can cost thousands of dollars over the course of a year. Family dinners in a nice restaurant are great for treats and celebrations, but too many of them will chip at your savings. If you work in a downtown office building or other urban area, eating out is a huge temptation as well. It's fast, close, and easy but not cheap. Pack a lunch, make dinners at home, and watch your savings increase in a very short period of time.

9. **Revisit your bills.** You pay bills for everything: insurance, cable, cell phone, subscriptions, kids programs, and more. First, take a good look at the bills you are paying. Do you need all these services? If so, do you need them with all the bells and whistles? Can you get away with reducing some services while still maintaining your needs? Try negotiating with your cable and phone provider or look for cheaper options. The costs of these services can be reduced with a few phone calls and comparative online shopping.

10. **Save tax refunds, bonuses, and gifts.** Sometimes we muddle our bonuses and gifts in with our other finances. We spend them quickly, use them to pay off other bills, or just lose track of them. A good method to increase savings, much like the "paying yourself first" method, is to immediately save all (if you can) or a portion of these funds back into your retirement fund. You'll be surprised at how much money can be accumulated with a few extra checks going back into your savings account.

Investors who started late and relied on markets to carry them into retirement lost much of their savings during that time. A one-time, albeit catastrophic, volatile economic event wiped them out, and many were forced to continue working after retirement. Part of the sad story is that many people did not have jobs to go back to, given the depths and length of the recession.

Not many people could have predicted the Great Recession; however, investors who started investing earlier and grew their assets over a longer period of time would have had a greater cushion from which to bounce back. Their investments would have been better able to withstand volatile market events over longer periods of time.

In today's world, there is an app for everything. Here are a few apps that have been reviewed in *The New York Times* that can help you with budgeting and financing.

- **BillGuard:** What started as a security service now has a spending analytics tool and personalized saving alerts. You are able to get a quick look at your monthly spending. Every time you swipe a credit card, the transaction is categorized for you.

- **Mint:** Mint is considered a comprehensive tool that allows you to keep tabs on your net worth and chart it with pie or bar charts for different time periods. A starter budget can be created based on up to three months' spending history with various categories, such as phone and groceries. The budget can be customized, and you can set up alerts to notify you if you've spent more than your budget allows.

- **You Need a Budget:** This app uses a Cloud Sync function that allows you to import information quickly. The method behind the app has four rules: give every dollar a job, save for a rainy day, roll with the punches, and live on last month's income.

- **Mvelopes:** This app gives you the power to allocate money to different "envelopes." Once you run out of money in each envelope, you either stop spending or take money to replenish it from another envelope. Transactions can be added manually, or you can connect to your accounts using the app's own technology.

TABLE 2.1: TRACKING YOUR INCOME AND EXPENSES

The only way to track your income and expenses is to write it down and compare what you are taking in versus what you are spending. Combine your income and expenses with your spouse's to get a better picture of the household, and see where any "leaks" are occurring. A simple spreadsheet makes your finances easy to track.

Monthly Income	Monthly Expenses	Employer Retirement Plan	Personal Retirement Plan	Other Savings

- **Spendee:** Simple manual input of your transactions allows you to see what you are spending and where the money is going. Spendee can back up data to iCloud, and the information can be exported.

- **BDGT:** Similar to Spendee, BDGT will give you a daily budget and a weekly allowance, thereby helping you, according to their website, spend less and save more.

The "Three-Legged Stool" of Retirement

Like any endeavor involving strategy and time, retirement planning should be tackled from many angles. What does this mean for you?

There used to be a time, and for many it still is, when Social Security was a sole retirement-funding strategy. Work, pay into the system, and get a pension when you are 65. It was straightforward and simple, but it was never meant to be the sole retirement solution for Americans. Also, there was a time when DB plans were more prevalent, and a worker who spent their entire career with one company could rely on a guaranteed pension at the end of their service.

But times have changed. Since 2010, the expenses of Social Security have exceeded its revenue. Also, by 2033, the reserves of Social Security will be depleted. After 2031, while still receiving tax revenue, there will only be enough to pay about three-quarters of the people requiring benefits.

So, Social Security has its funding issues, DB plans are dwindling, and the expectation is that you must choose from your employer's DC options. This is where the **"three-legged stool"** comes in.

Any stool, in order to support itself, must have at least three legs. The same is true for your retirement fund. Any single option mentioned previously will not fully accomplish financial goals on its own. Your retirement "stool," the one that needs to support you (and probably a spouse) must consist of three saving elements. They are the following: Social Security, employer savings plan, and personal savings.

According to the 2013 report by the Employee Benefit Research Institute, Social Security for people 65 and older accounts for the largest part of their income, at 40 percent. The same report shows that pensions and annuities account for about 20 percent of income. However, that tide is shifting. As DB plans disappear and you are asked to manage more of your own retirement savings, income may be more evenly split or tipped more toward your retirement plans rather than the government. Lower income workers still rely heavily on Social Security and likely will for some time.

Within personal savings, there are many tax-deferred options such as IRAs, **Roth IRAs**, and plans for the self-employed, which will be discussed more in step 3. Some companies have options that allow you to contribute more than your plan allows, with features for you to make after-tax contributions that grow on a tax-deferred basis. There are also deferred annuities.

These investments are tax-deferred, which means you will not generally be taxed until you make a withdrawal. The premise is that, in retirement, you are in a lower tax bracket, and the tax you pay on the withdrawals will be less than if you used the money during your working years.

The "Three-Bucket" Strategy

Norbert Mindel might not exactly be a household name, but if you're reading this book and serious about your retirement, you should get to know his thoughts on investment strategies. Mindel is a principal at Forum Financial Management, LP, in Chicago. In 2010, he published a book titled *Wealth Management in the New Economy: Investor Strategies for Growing, Protecting, and Transferring Wealth*.

Mindel suggests putting money into three separate buckets. The **"three-bucket" strategy** can be a way to help nervous investors who fear stock markets and losing their savings close to retirement.

- **Bucket #1:** Shorter-term and emergency savings. Put cash in the first bucket for living expenses.

- **Bucket #2:** Longer-term and annual income savings. Invest 80 percent in investment-grade bonds and the rest in diversified stock funds. When savings from Bucket #1 diminish, money from the second bucket can be used.

- **Bucket #3:** Long-term growth savings. Invest 60 percent in stocks and 40 percent in bonds. This is the fail-safe bucket that helps replenish the first two buckets.

THREE-BUCKET STRATEGY: HOW IT WORKS

Let's say retiree Sam has saved $2 million toward his retirement and wants to spend 4 percent of that per year to maintain an income of $80,000. In that scenario, Bucket #1 would need $240,000 invested in money market funds or certificates of deposit, essentially enough cash to cover three years of living expenses.

When Bucket #1 starts to get too low, money from Bucket #2 can be used to replenish it. Mindel would say Bucket #2 should hold about $500,000. Bucket #3 would have about $1 million.

Now, let's assume stock values in Bucket #3 drop 40 to 50 percent as they did during the Great Recession. The "three-bucket" strategy would provide Sam with enough assets in the first two buckets to last 10 years. According to Mindel, stocks and bonds will likely return about 7 percent per year during the next 10 years. With that, Bucket #3 would double to $2 million and be enough to refill the other buckets and protect his savings from inflation.

Mindel proposes a fourth bucket if you are risk-averse and a nervous investor. This bucket represents the following three types of risk protection:

1. **Longevity and point-in-time risks.** This protects you against outliving your resources.

2. **Long-term care insurance.** This will fund the risks of needing a nursing facility or at-home health services.

3. **Family protection.** This can replace lost wages, portfolio losses, or funding estate taxes, for example.

In the book, Mindel uses a three-step formula to help people analyze their retirement cash flow and how much they need to allocate against longevity risks. He says you should list expenses and determine your "essential living" and discretionary living expenses. Then, list your guaranteed sources of income and subtract your expenses from that. Mindel concludes that once you've covered your expenses you can create a more predictable income "stream" from your other three buckets, which "will be the foundation for your retirement lifestyle."

What to Do and When

Whether you are starting out on your retirement-savings journey or nearing the end, it's helpful to look at your life in stages and see when it makes sense to accomplish certain retirement-savings milestones. The following is a rough guide of when to reach these milestones.

Your 20s

It's true that after graduation, if you are lucky enough to find a job quickly, you will have debts to pay. You will contend with student loans, getting your own place, getting a car, possibly getting married, and a whole host of other money-spending endeavors. However, it's also the time to start thinking about retirement savings. As you have learned, the earlier you start, the better off you will be, and the less catching up you will have to do.

It's hard to think about retiring when you are in your 20s. You've barely worked a day in your life, and your career may change directions many times. Still, building a foundation for your financial future and learning good habits, including budgeting, will benefit you in the long run. Opening your first savings account and investing in mutual funds, for example, will help you benefit from the compounding effect discussed earlier in this step. Don't be afraid to get started at what seems like a very early stage of your working life.

Consumer and commercial financial provider Wells Fargo provides a checklist for each retirement stage. The following is the checklist for people in their 20s:

- Enroll in your workplace retirement plan.
- Create an IRA.
- Build an emergency fund.
- Create a budget.
- Keep debt under control.
- Make sure you are on track (i.e., by using retirement calculators).

Your 30s

By the time you've reached your 30s, you may have established yourself to some degree in a career with a steady job, or you have started your own business. You may have a family, and some of your priorities may have changed. By now, you should be thinking about your mortgage payments, getting out of debt or lessening your debt, possibly creating a second income stream, and ensuring your pension savings are going in the right direction.

The following is the Wells Fargo checklist for people in their 30s:

- Maximize tax-advantaged retirement accounts.
- Aim to save 10 percent of your income.
- Consider adding bonuses or other payments to your retirement savings.
- Build (or continue building) an emergency fund.
- Keep debt down.
- Refine your plan if necessary (e.g., check investment allocations).

Your 40s

Your 30s and 40s are your best earning years, so it is important to have a solid plan in place to take advantage of this stage in your life. You may be saving money for vacations, considering how to pay for the costs of education, and looking for ways to further reduce your debt.

The following is the Wells Fargo checklist for people in their 40s:

- Review your retirement plan.
- Protect yourself and your family (e.g., update beneficiaries in your will).
- Manage your employer-sponsored plans if you change jobs.
- Take advantage of the tax benefits of retirement plans.
- Figure out how long your savings will last.
- Strengthen your emergency fund.
- Take care of your high-interest debt.

Your 50s and 60s

By this stage of your life, you are well advanced in your career and/or are looking at the exit strategy from your business. Your kids may be grown, and again, your financial priorities have changed. Some of your spending and saving might be related to helping pay off your child's education costs and looking after aging parents. You will want to take a hard look at your investment portfolio if changes are needed.

The following is the Wells Fargo checklist for people in their 50s and 60s:

- Catch up on retirement contributions.
- Ensure your **asset allocation** aligns with your goals.
- Consider additional life insurance protection.
- Identify sources of retirement income.
- Assess what your monthly expenses will be.
- Create or review a withdrawal strategy.
- Simplify your finances to better track assets and manage spending.

Your 70s and Beyond

These are your retirement years—the years you've been saving for all this time, and hopefully you have followed a plan to get to this point. By this stage, your time and money will be spent on lifestyle and living expenses, travel and hobbies you've been holding off on, creating a legacy for your kids, and ensuring your will provides a proper and protected distribution strategy.

The following is the Wells Fargo checklist for people in their 70s and older:

- Review your finances with a professional financial advisor.
- Make the most of your retirement income plan (i.e., ensure your income will last, look at other products such as annuities, etc.).
- Reevaluate your estate needs (e.g., update beneficiaries if necessary, prepare for long-term healthcare needs, inform family and loved ones where to locate important documents, and so on).

These lists are certainly not exhaustive and will be different for everyone depending on factors such as how much you save, how much debt you have accrued, and how much your earn. However, the concepts are universal and speak to the need for planning and preparing your entire life. From the moment you start your first job to the moment you retire, proper and appropriate planning at each life milestone will make your retirement easier to navigate.

As you move ahead on this journey, you'll learn more details about the investment types that fit into the plan and how to use them to your maximum advantage.

STEP

INVEST WISELY

There's good news and bad news when you look at your retirement savings plans and goals. The good news is that you have more control over your savings. The bad news is that you have more control over your savings.

What does this mean? With the decline of DB plans and the increase of DC plans, investors are being asked to take charge of their investment decisions, investment management, and overall trajectory of their investments more than they did in the past. It's good news because you have a say in where your money can go and how much risk, for example, you are willing to tolerate. However, most Americans are not equipped with the knowledge, time, or desire to manage their funds, and they often run into obstacles that negatively affect their savings. That is why the good and bad news is the same thing.

After you've carefully assessed your goals and dreams and created budgets and savings plans that automatically deduct funds into an account, you still have to decide where the money is best invested. Not only that, you have to understand your own risk aversions and what the best investments are for your stage of life and know whether you are looking for growth, income, or maintenance. There is no end to the questions you need to answer in order to best invest your funds for maximum returns.

The first step is getting a basic understanding of some of the types of investments available.

Common Investment Properties

If you've ever watched a business channel on television, you have a company 401(k) plan or IRA, or if you know anyone who does, you've already seen the thousands of investment choices available to the average American. Wall Street used to be isolated and basically a club (which it mostly still is), but Americans are investing more in the markets and looking for income growth in areas they may have never considered before.

According to 2014 data from the Investment Company Institute, there is approximately $15 trillion invested in mutual funds. This does not include individual stocks, bonds, real estate, and other more risky investments. The Gallup organization found that 54 percent of Americans are invested in either stocks or mutual funds. Part of this rise is due to the types of retirement savings vehicles available but also the fact that the economy has been in a low interest rate environment for some time.

Americans are looking for healthy returns on their investments, and the old days of savings accounts are not meeting their needs. What are some of the investment options available today?

Stocks

At its very basic level, a stock is a unit of ownership in a particular company. Often, when companies grow to a certain level on their own revenue but want to expand faster and with greater strength, they will raise money by offering partial ownership in the company and issue shares of stock.

As America was expanding westward in the 1800s, many of the railroad companies would issue stock to help pay for expansion. Mining companies would do the same. As a part owner of a company, you have a say in its operations, although that is limited given the way public companies are run. You are also entitled to vote on company decisions, in some cases, and you are allotted a share of the company's earnings. Stocks are traded on an open market. In the United States, the New York Stock Exchange, NASDAQ, and mercantile exchanges, for example, are free markets that allow individual and large investors (often pension funds) to buy and sell their stocks.

There are two types of stocks investors can own: preferred and common. **Preferred stock** usually does not give investors the ability to vote but allows them to have higher claims on assets and earnings. **Common stock**, alternatively, gives investors voting rights on some management decisions but less priority on assets (e.g., in the event that a company is liquidated).

Some stocks also pay dividends, which is a portion of the company's revenue distributed to investors. The board of directors generally decides the amount. Many investors like dividend-paying stocks as a regular source of income that can be used for further savings, reinvestment to accumulate more stock, or as pocket money for day-to-day expenses.

Since 1926, the average stock has earned 10 percent per year and remained a relatively solid investment for retirement savings plans. However, down markets can occur, and, since World War II, there have been eight such down cycles. The key message here is that stocks, like most other investments, should be considered a long-term investment. It is not wise to buy or sell on immediate economic news or news of a company in question.

Bonds

Whereas companies can raise money by selling small pieces of the company to investors via stock ownership, sometimes the decision is made to borrow money instead. The company will issue bonds, which are a form of debt incurred by the company seeking money. Perhaps you or someone you know has government or municipal bonds (also known as treasuries), or you have given them as gifts for graduation. In these cases, the government borrows money from you with the promise of paying you back at a certain time with a certain interest rate. You act as a bank. The government will generally use the money for infrastructure projects or other funding gaps for which they might need a shorter-term finance solution.

Bonds are generally considered "safer" than stocks because they produce a steady stream of interest income, as opposed to stocks, which are more volatile. However, like any investment, they come with risks. Corporations will issue bonds, and the less credit-worthy they are, the higher the interest rate or "yield." These bonds are often referred to as "junk bonds." You are rewarded for your risks but may lose a lot of your money for the same reasons.

Bonds with longer time horizons pay higher yields because you are being paid for letting the borrower use your money for a longer period of time. Interest rates are one of the biggest influencers on bond prices. As rates go up, bond prices decline. Why? Generally, the newer bonds will be issued with higher interest rates, making current bonds with lower rates less valuable.

Mutual Funds

One of the more common investments for individuals, especially within retirement plans, is mutual funds. A mutual fund will take money from other investors, pool it together, and invest it in stocks, bonds, or other investment vehicles on behalf of its investors. This benefits the investor in a variety of ways:

- **Professional investment management:** One of the key benefits of choosing a mutual fund versus buying your own stocks and bonds is the professional investment management the issuing company is providing. Managers select the investments, monitor the investments, and make day-to-day decisions on their growth and strategy for continued success. This is not to say you couldn't do this yourself or that investment managers are infallible; however, they do provide the average investor with some peace of mind and professional attention to the investment for a fee.

- **Diversification:** Every fund invests in a variety of investments. Even if the fund follows a particular strategy (e.g., international blue-chip companies), there is still a diverse selection of stocks within the fund. Hopefully this **diversification** reduces volatility because the investments are spread out rather than clustered into one company. If you own one or two stocks in a particular industry and that industry has a downturn, you can expect to lose a lot of money. If you own 100 stocks spread throughout a variety of industries, one or two down-cycles in a particular industry will not affect the others, and you will preserve your capital. It may even grow if the other investments are doing well.

- **Potential for long-term growth:** Every fund, no matter what its strategy or focus, can help you build a portfolio of investments that generates long-term growth. Some funds seek to generate regular income, and others will generate shorter-term income. Either way, the overall picture is that your portfolio is a longer-term one, much like individual invest-ments, that should not be bought and sold depending on the day's news.

Target-Date/Life-Cycle Funds

There has been a movement over the last decade or so to give people more investment choices that target their specific stage in life. For example, younger investors, who have years ahead of them before retirement, can afford investments that take on more risk and can weather market cycles.

As you age, your time horizon narrows, and the gap between your work-ing years and retirement decreases. You have less time to weather cycles, and your tolerance for risk should also decrease. In other words, you have gone through the growth phase of investing. The older you get, the more you need to preserve that growth. This is how **target-date/life-cycle funds** work. Different funds offer different risk/growth/preservation strategies depend-ing on how old you are. Some 401(k)s will provide life-cycle funds that rebalance your portfolio for you, depending on your stage of life. For some plans, you simply select as your situation changes.

Exchange-Traded Funds

Exchange-traded funds (ETFs) are funds that follow indexes such as the New York Stock Exchange. The main difference between ETFs and other types of index funds is that ETFs are only interested in replicating the performance of the index they track. They don't try to beat the market like some other index funds.

As opposed to the professional management benefit of some mutual funds, ETFs are more of a passive investment. Only minor adjustments are made to keep the fund in line with its index, but this is why they are cheaper to purchase than actively managed funds. Also, because fewer trades are made on passively managed funds, there is less potential for high capital gains costs.

Mutual funds and variations of these funds have grown, and the choices are endless. Investments range from following a stock index to certain industries, certain size stocks, or bonds; different geographic areas; develop-ing versus developed economies; and even socially responsible funds that, in addition to looking to make money for their investors, they also invest with a conscience (e.g., no tobacco).

Real Estate

For most people, buying and owning their homes is the largest real estate purchase they will ever make. However, real estate, which is a relatively easy investment for people to understand and see the benefits of, is becoming a popular choice for growing income. The Gallup organization found that 25 percent of Americans rate real estate the best long-term investment, essentially tying with gold (24 percent of Americans say gold is the best long-term investment). Why?

There are a few reasons why investors like real estate for their retirement (or other) long-term goals.

- **Post–Great Recession:** Real estate prices and values took a dramatic tumble in the Great Recession of 2007–2009. Housing construction was also on a steep decline. In 2008, the number of housing units under construction was 780,900. However, by 2009, it dropped to 495,400 units. During the next four years, it averaged more than 40 percent less than in 2008.

  But that was then. In the summer of 2014, spending on US construction showed strong signs of recovery, rising by the largest amount in more than two years. All major categories of construction made gains.

- **Steady streams of income:** Besides the value of the actual asset(s) in real estate, there is often an income component to the investment. If it is a large commercial project, rents or leases provide income. If it is a rental apartment complex or smaller housing unit, the same holds true. Investors appreciate these steadier and usually less volatile forms of income in their portfolios.

Within real estate, there are diverse options for investors. For example, much like a typical mutual fund, you can find options that offer investments in commercial real estate in a particular region or part of the world, residential and apartment rental units, shopping malls, or a combination. There are subcategories that involve warehousing and logistics sites as well.

Sometimes these investments can be made directly into particular companies that manage such properties. They also can be invested through a **real estate investment trust (REIT)**. A REIT acts like a mutual fund and allows anyone to invest in portfolios of properties the same way they might invest in a portfolio of stocks. The benefit to individual investors is that you do not need to finance or actively manage properties yourself. The REIT does that for you. It's an active management strategy that allows you access to large-scale real estate holdings.

There are two types of REITs: equity and mortgage. **Equity REITs** get most of their revenue from rent. **Mortgage REITs** get most of their revenue from interest on mortgages or mortgage-backed securities.

Gold

As mentioned earlier, gold essentially ties with real estate as the best long-term investment for Americans, according to the Gallup organization. Although the price has dropped off a bit from its peak in 2011, it still remains high and has often been considered a "safe haven" hedge against other currencies or economic strife. The decline in its attractiveness recently has more to do with the rebound in stocks and real estate.

Private Equity

Private equity is a relatively new investment type for individual investors and retirees. Many large pension funds and wealthier investors have known about private equity for some time. Essentially, these are investments that are not public (companies that do not issue stock or trade on open markets). Your investment is not very liquid, meaning it cannot be retrieved too quickly because it is more difficult to find buyers and sellers within the private equity market than in open public markets.

Private equity includes investments in start-up companies or in any company that needs capital but has not issued stocks to raise funds. This can be a very long-term investment, and because of its illiquidity, it is not as beneficial to retirees. However, many large investment management firms are attempting to make private equity products available to DC plans. This investment option is still in its infancy and not as widespread as mutual fund investments.

This list of investment options is not exhaustive, and each investment discussed comes with different nuances. However, the list represents the majority of investments you might find available through a financial advisor or workplace pension plan.

Defined Benefit Versus Defined Contribution Plans

Throughout this book, there have been brief explanations and discussions surrounding different types of pension plans. There are two basic kinds: the defined benefit (DB) plan and the defined contribution (DC) plan.

The Defined Benefit Plan

One of the first recorded pension plans in America was created by the American Express Company in 1875. That model has not changed much over time.

The DB plan is a predetermined payment made to you upon leaving or retiring from a particular job. A formula usually made up of years of service, your age, and your salary determines what you will receive. Your employer manages the assets with little to no involvement on your part. Until the early 1970s, pension plans were not a protected benefit. For example, in 1963, the Studebaker auto company let its employees go, and more than 4,000 workers in South Bend, Indiana, lost some or all of their pensions.

In 1974, President Gerald Ford signed the Employee Retirement Income Security Act into law, which created the Pension Benefit Guaranty Corporation, a pension insurance program that guaranteed workers' pension benefits.

According to 2014 data from the Investment Company Institute, the national association of US investment companies, private sector DB pension plans hold about $3.0 trillion.

The Defined Contribution Plan

In 1978, the Internal Revenue Service (IRS) included a provision that became Internal Revenue Code section 401(k), for which many plans are named. The code stated that employees are not to be taxed on the portion of income they choose to put aside as deferred compensation, as opposed to immediate cash payments. One of the first companies to create a 401(k) or DC plan was Johnson & Johnson in 1979.

The income you receive from a DC plan at retirement is not predetermined. You will make contributions to the plan, and in some cases, your employer might match your contribution to a certain percentage of your salary. The money that is set aside is invested into investment choices made by you.

There are other types of DC plans such as stock-sharing plans, simplified employee plans, 457s, and the 403(b), all of which are tax-deferred-type plans for different sectors and/or industries.

According to a review of investment trends from the Investment Company Institute:

> *The largest components of retirement assets were IRAs and employer-sponsored DC plans, holding $6.5 trillion and $5.9 trillion, respectively, at year-end 2013. Other employer-sponsored plans include private-sector DB pension funds ($3.0 trillion), state and local government employee retirement plans ($3.9 trillion), and federal government plans—which include both federal employees' DB plans and the Thrift Savings Plan ($1.8 trillion). In addition, annuity reserves outside of retirement plans were $2.0 trillion at year-end 2013.*

Personal Retirement Plans

Individual Retirement Account

An IRA is usually set up through your bank or some other financial institution. It allows you as an individual to save for retirement on a tax-deferred basis, as opposed to saving through your employer.

When you leave a job, change jobs, or retire, IRAs are considered a good place to roll over your retirement savings for a relatively seamless transition and to avoid tax penalties. Some employers also allow you to keep your retirement savings in their 401(k) plans until distribution occurs.

Roth Individual Retirement Account

With Roth IRAs, you are not eligible for up-front tax deductions, but Roth withdrawals are tax-free. The money is yours and not a tax-subsidized contribution from the government, so you can take out your contributions at any time with no penalties and no tax implications.

Roth IRAs make the most sense if you expect your tax rate to be higher during retirement than your current rate. That makes Roth IRAs sound savings vehicles for young, lower-income workers who won't mind not getting the upfront tax deduction and who will benefit from years of tax-free, compounded growth. Roth IRAs also appeal to those people who want to lower their taxes in retirement, as well as to older, wealthier taxpayers who want to leave assets to their heirs that are tax-free.

The Differences: Defined Benefit Versus Defined Contribution

There are distinct differences to each savings vehicle that can be good or bad, depending on your point of view.

Defined Benefit (DB) Plan	Defined Contribution (DC) Plan
Takes less effort on your part and requires little or no investment knowledge	Requires you to select your investments and have some understanding of the markets
A "guaranteed" pension after retirement	Can fluctuate and have no predetermined outcome
Costs more for an employer to manage	Costs less for an employer to manage while reducing their liabilities at the same time
Managed by an employer or an investment management firm requiring little input on your part	Requires investment knowledge; may also require you to seek outside help from investment advisors/professionals

How to Create a Risk-Adjusted Portfolio

Earlier in this step, you learned how your tolerance for risk can, and should, depend on your age and the point you are at in your career. With a greater time horizon comes the ability to withstand greater volatility, and with a smaller one, the opposite is true. Whatever your stage is in life, your portfolio needs to be balanced so it carries the "right amount" of risk versus reward. Risk adjustment is a never-ending exercise. You must constantly be monitoring your investments to make sure they are meeting your needs at a particular time.

How do you do this? Through diversification. One of the keys to avoiding too much risk is to not put all your eggs in one basket. Different parts of the market will rise and fall at different intervals for different reasons. If your portfolio is diversified enough by having some risk, some conservative investments, and even some cash, you are more likely to feel less volatility than if you had all your money in a risky portfolio when times were bad or bond funds when the stock market was doing well.

INVESTMENT STRATEGIES: PROS AND CONS

No single strategy is best. Your age, stage in life, expenses, debt, savings, and tolerance for risk all play into which strategies will work best for you. Even when you've decided on a retirement strategy, it will need to be revisited and rebalanced over time. The following is a list of pros and cons of some popular investment strategies.

STOCKS

Pros: They have long-term growth potential and are an understandable investment, with easy-to-measure gains and losses and the ability to generate income through dividends. Investor owns a portion of a corporation.

Cons: It can be difficult to manage a large portfolio. They are volatile, with no guarantee of earnings, and there are costs for administration and trading.

BONDS

Pros: They can be more secure than stocks, with guaranteed income and can help balance a portfolio with other investments. Bonds are a long-term investment that is easy to understand. Growth is easy to calculate, the principal is maintained (unlike stocks), and bonds are averse to risk. Debt holders generally get paid before shareholders in bankruptcy situations.

Cons: Bonds have limited growth potential, work only for the most conservative investors, and are reactionary to movement in interest rates.

ETFs

Pros: They involve low costs (compared to other funds), require no minimum investment, have tax advantages over mutual funds, and provide diversification to a portfolio.

Cons: They can be tempting to trade frequently because they trade on the stock exchange and are volatile (like stocks). Some only trade once a day, and some ETFs use expensive and volatile derivatives to create contracts.

(continued)

INVESTMENT STRATEGIES: PROS AND CONS

(continued from previous page)

401(K) PLAN

Pros: A 401(k) plan is an employer plan that allows employees to save for retirement. The company often matches the employee's contribution to a certain percentage. The plan enables employees to have control over their investment selections and is relatively easy to navigate and understand. Sometimes the funds are transferable to the employee's next job's plan or can be rolled into private retirement savings.

Cons: The plan forces you to manage your investments; there is no guaranteed retirement income. Sometimes the employer provides too little (or sometimes too much) information, which can lead to confusion. Costs of administration are sometimes handed down to the employee.

DEFINED BENEFIT (DB) PLAN

Pros: This plan guarantees income upon retirement, with little or no investment knowledge needed on the employee's part; the employer administers the plan.

Cons: The employee is reliant on company management of plan, with no matching contributions. The funds can be reduced when the employer is going through rough times.

Please note the following three "model" portfolios for aggressive, moderate, and conservative investors. Conventional wisdom will tell you that the younger you are, the more aggressive you should be with your investments. Time is on your side. As you get older, you need to rebalance, reduce your risk, and revisit how your portfolio is diversified as you preserve capital but still look for investments that will grow your income.

Within the most aggressive portfolio, equity/stock-type investments make up a whopping 95 percent of the portfolio. As you move to moderate allocation, equity investments make up 60 percent of the portfolio. At the most conservative level, equities make up 15 percent of the portfolio. This tells us two things: (1) Rebalancing will occur from stocks to bonds or fixed income investments, and (2) even within each portfolio, there is still a diversification of investments to ensure you are not getting hurt by one sector when others are doing well.

MODEL INVESTMENT PORTFOLIOS

AGGRESSIVE ALLOCATION

INVESTMENT IN EQUITIES	42-YEAR GROWTH ON $10K INVESTMENT	BEST-YEAR RETURN

95% $520k

+39.9% ▲

WORST-YEAR RETURN

−36.0% ▼

Aggressive allocation is best for those who: (1) are most concerned with investments growing in value, (2) don't need current income, and (3) have a good tolerance for a higher degree of risk.

50%	20%	25%	5%
LARGE-COMPANY EQUITY	SMALL-COMPANY EQUITY	INTERNATIONAL EQUITY	CASH & CASH INVESTMENTS

MODERATE ALLOCATION

INVESTMENT IN EQUITIES	42-YEAR GROWTH ON $10K INVESTMENT	BEST-YEAR RETURN

60% $463k

+30.9% ▲

WORST-YEAR RETURN

−20.9% ▼

Moderate allocation is best for those who: (1) want solid growth with relative stability, (2) don't need current income, and (3) can tolerate some fluctuations but want considerable less risk than overall stock market.

35%	10%	15%	35%	5%
LARGE-COMPANY EQUITY	SMALL-COMPANY EQUITY	INTERNATIONAL EQUITY	FIXED INCOME	CASH & CASH INVESTMENTS

CONSERVATIVE ALLOCATION

INVESTMENT IN EQUITIES	42-YEAR GROWTH ON $10K INVESTMENT	BEST-YEAR RETURN

20% $257k

+22.8% ▲

WORST-YEAR RETURN

−4.6% ▼

Conservative allocation is best for those who: (1) want current income and stability and (2) want capital preservation.

15%	5%	50%	30%
LARGE-COMPANY EQUITY	INTERNATIONAL EQUITY	FIXED INCOME	CASH & CASH INVESTMENTS

SOURCE: Adapted from Charles Schwab

Which Plan Is the Right One?

DC plans, DB plans, IRAs, and individual savings all have a place in your retirement strategy, and each of them provides different types of retirement savings opportunities. Sometimes it's as simple as just using what you have. If your employer offers a 401(k) plan with a match, then that's the right one for you. If you are still lucky enough to have a DB plan, then that's the right plan.

IRAs and Roth IRAs are part of the personal savings plan strategy that was mentioned when discussing the "three-legged stool" of retirement. It's a means of adding to your savings in a tax-deferred way to help you maximize your savings potential. Having several plans increases your savings and helps you with risk adjustments. The more money you can save in a variety of investments, the better off you will be.

For example, if your 401(k) offers limited investment selections, you can offset that imbalance with a well-diversified IRA portfolio. Generally, if you've maxed out contributions toward your employer-sponsored plan and received the full matching contribution, it is a good time to look for diversification through other plans. There is no right or wrong solution as long as you are saving and monitoring your investments properly.

Knowing where to invest and determining which vehicle best suits your needs takes time and patience. You'll want to know what you don't know, so you can seek the proper guidance and make decisions that work for your retirement needs. Financial planners can help with that task, but understanding the basics of your plan(s) and the investment selections is also necessary. You have choices, and that is a good thing in most cases. Take advantage of the selections available, know your stage in life, and know the risk you are willing to take to achieve your greatest rewards.

As we move on, we will start looking at the end of the cycle and how to begin distributions and withdrawals from your plan.

CHOOSING THE RIGHT FINANCIAL PLANNER

The importance of saving for retirement should never be underestimated. In many cases, especially as you are asked to take more control of your decision making, you may need the help of financial professionals. Many Americans have a tough time with the idea of financial planners. In the 2012 Household Financial Planning Survey prepared for the Certified Financial Planner Board of Standards and the Consumer Federation of America, 55 percent of Americans said, "It's hard for me to know whom to trust for financial advice." Also, the survey found that 52 percent of people said, "To me, investing seems complicated," and 55 percent said, "I'm worried about losing my money if I invest it."

So how do you choose a financial planner that's right for you?

- **Look at the planner's designation.** Are they certified to do what they say they do? Certified financial planners (CFPs) receive rigorous training and education to get their designations. They also commit to continuing that education both in finance and ethics in order to maintain their CFP status.

- **Look at his or her compensation structure.** Does the financial planner offer advice or services on a commission basis, or does he or she charge a flat fee? There is no right choice, but you should be comfortable with how the advisor you choose gets paid. Commission-based advisors get paid on trades and stock transactions, and they can have a bias toward particular stocks or sectors (but not all do).

- **Determine if he or she will act as a fiduciary.** Some planners will take a pledge to act in the client's best interest at all times. Those who are not fiduciaries will sell you products that are "suitable" but not necessarily in your best interest at all times.

- **Ask someone you trust.** Perhaps a relative or friend of yours has insight into financial planning and uses somebody for his or her investment management needs. Getting a referral from someone you know is often the best way to find trustworthy planners who will do their best to take care of your finances.

The Certified Financial Planner Board of Standards (www.cfp.net) and National Association of Personal Financial Advisors (www.nafpa.org) are good starting points for researching financial planners, what they do, and where to find them.

10 QUESTIONS TO ASK YOUR FINANCIAL PLANNER

1. What is your designation: Are you a certified financial planner?

2. What is your fee structure: Is it commission-based or a flat fee?

3. Are you a "fiduciary" financial planner?

4. What is your experience?

5. What are your areas of expertise?

6. What is your overall approach to financial planning?

7. Will you be working with me, or do you have a team of advisors?

8. Can I see a sample financial plan? (This can help you form other questions about what is appropriate or not for your personal financial plan.)

9. What makes your client experience unique?

10. How much interaction do you have with your clients?

STEP

WITHDRAW STRATEGICALLY

This might be the point in your life you've been waiting for. You've saved, diversified, and grown your retirement savings, and it's time to retire and withdraw your savings. However, you may need to withdraw funds for personal reasons or emergencies. Maybe you think your retirement savings is a good place to get a down payment for your next home.

Always remember that early withdrawals from your retirement savings accounts have consequences. For this reason, you should consider an early withdrawal as a last resort. Your ability to benefit from compounding or other positive savings attributes, as well as your entire future potential retirement fund, could be put into jeopardy.

Emergency Funds

A concept that has not been discussed yet is the need for emergency funds. The "three-bucket" rule comes close, in that the second and third buckets are meant to help replenish depleted funds in the first bucket. However, this is more in line with saving for retirement.

Having an emergency fund is something to seriously consider along with your retirement savings. Many financial experts believe a three- to six-month cushion will carry you through job losses, illness, or other unforeseen circumstances and help bridge any dry periods in your earnings.

In a 2011 survey by the National Foundation for Credit Counseling, the oldest nonprofit financial counseling organization in the United States, 64 percent of Americans essentially said they do not have enough money in their savings accounts to handle a $1,000 emergency. Think about it. If you have a minor car accident, your hot water heater breaks down, or you need to fix anything, it could easily cost at least $1,000. What would you do then? Tapping into your retirement savings will cost you money in penalties, so this would not be the best decision.

The first order of business is to have some kind of emergency fund to handle unexpected expenses or losses of employment that don't last too long. This is a good time to take another look at your budget and needs versus wants. If at all possible, cuts should be made so that emergency funding can be stored away and you don't need to use your retirement savings.

Another option is to take some money (only if you absolutely have to for an emergency) as you roll over your employment retirement plans into IRAs. If you take a payout, your employer will withhold 20 percent of the taxable portion for federal income taxes. Also, if you are younger than 59 1/2, you might have to pay a 10 percent early withdrawal fee on the taxable part of the distribution you take. There could be state and local taxes taken out as well. An option could be to take out a portion of what you need rather than the entire balance. You'd save a bit on penalties, not jeopardize your entire savings fund, and still have some cash to pay the debt you need the money for.

Retirement Withdrawals

Of course, you may actually be retiring, so your need for the distribution of funds is perfectly legitimate and will not be subject to any penalties. How do you know when to withdraw the funds, and what do you need to think about differently from when you were saving for retirement?

Let's start with the government.

According to IRS rules and regulations, when you reach age 70 1/2, you must begin withdrawing funds from your retirement plan on an annual basis unless you are still working. That is the law, and you don't really have a say in the matter.

IRAs are a slightly different story. **Required minimum distributions (RMDs)** must begin once you reach 70 1/2 regardless of whether or not you've retired. With retirement savings plans or IRAs, it is up to you to take the correct amount of RMDs on time every year, or you will face penalties for noncompliance. Overall, your age and retirement savings account value determine the amount you must withdraw.

A retirement RMD calculator is available from the Financial Industry Regulatory Authority (see Resources, page 134).

You are allowed to take more than the RMD each year if your plan has a flexible withdrawal arrangement. If you take less for any reason or if the required annual withdrawal isn't made before the end of the year, you will face penalties.

There are basically two ages that are important to consider when you are looking at withdrawals from your retirement savings plans: 59 1/2 and 70 1/2. The first age is generally the age at which you can take money from your tax-deferred savings plan without incurring a 10 percent early withdrawal tax, so long as you've left your job. The second age is the one which you must begin taking mandatory withdrawals, although you actually have until April 1 following the year you turn 70 1/2 to take the first withdrawal.

In many instances, you may withdraw from your 401(k) account or retirement savings account when you retire from your job, but you must be your employer's required retirement age. Some employers make you withdraw from your plan when you retire. Again, if that is the case, you have the option of rolling it over into an IRA.

If you're still working at 70 1/2, you can postpone withdrawals from your 401(k) until April 1 following the year you retire. The only time that does not apply is if you own at least 5 percent of the company. In a scenario where you are an owner, you can't postpone taking income and must begin withdrawals on the normal schedule.

The following chart shows the ages at which several retirement "events" will occur. Keeping these ages and milestones in mind throughout your retirement savings process can help you plan when it is best to begin withdrawal and the amount of money you will likely need. More will be discussed about Social Security and Medicare in later steps in this book.

Age	Retirement Event	Age	Retirement Event
59 ½	Penalty-free withdrawals	70	Social Security (late)
62	Social Security (early)	70 ½	Required withdrawals
65 ½	Medicare		

Hardship Withdrawals

There are times in life when large sums of money are required. For better or for worse, your retirement fund has a large portion of your savings locked into it. In these moments, the IRS does have provisions for you to take your money out with no penalty. Not all employers have this option because they are not required to do so.

The plan sponsor (your employer) will provide the criteria they determine for these hardship withdrawals. Although some plans may allow you to take your money to pay for a funeral or care for someone who is ill, they may not allow you to take a withdrawal for the purposes of buying a house. The criteria and reasons allowed for withdrawal are different for every plan, so it is best to check with your employer.

The IRS says the withdrawal must be made "on account of an immediate and heavy financial need of the employee and the amount must be necessary to satisfy the financial need."

What does that mean, specifically? The IRS explains it this way:

Certain expenses are deemed to be immediate and heavy, including:
(1) certain medical expenses; (2) costs relating to the purchase of a
principal residence; (3) tuition and related educational fees and expenses;
(4) payments necessary to prevent eviction from, or foreclosure on, a
principal residence; (5) burial or funeral expenses; and (6) certain expenses
for the repair of damage to the employee's principal residence.

Still, your retirement savings plan should not be considered your first choice for such events. Both the IRS and conventional wisdom will tell you that if you have other resources, even your spouse or from your children, you would not be allowed to take funds from your retirement plans. Keep in mind that hardship withdrawals are subject to income tax, and if you are younger than 59 ½, you would pay a 10 percent withdrawal penalty as well.

10 QUESTIONS TO ASK YOURSELF BEFORE WITHDRAWING RETIREMENT FUNDS

1. **Do I really need the money?**
   It seems like a simple question, but think about it before you withdraw your funds. There will be tax and penalties, and it will affect the long-term outcome of your investments. Maybe you have the extra resources somewhere else or maybe, if you think hard enough about it, you can forgo the withdrawal altogether. Think before you withdraw and make sure it is for a worthy cause.

2. **How far along am I in my retirement goals?**
   Consider your savings plan and the goals you are trying to achieve. Look at the amount of funds you have today versus what you think you will accumulate. Given all of that, do you have enough long-term time to catch up if you make a withdrawal?

3. **How disciplined are my savings habits?**
   The moment you decide to withdraw from your retirement plan, you should consider how you will replenish that money. Are you a good saver? Have you been consistently taking money and putting it away for retirement? Consider your own habits when making this decision.

4. **Does the withdrawal fall under the "hardship" category?**
   Sometimes you will need large sums of money that can only be tapped via your retirement plan. Make sure your reason(s) fall under a hardship categorization so that you are not penalized for the withdrawal.

5. **What does my employer allow regarding a hardship withdrawal?**
   Not all employer-sponsored retirement plans allow hardship withdrawals, and those that do have different criteria for making the withdrawal. Make sure you know what is covered within your employer's plan and if you can access the funds when necessary. Some issues the IRS says you should review are the following:

   - The procedures to receive a hardship distribution
   - The plan's definition of a hardship
   - Limits on the amount and type of funds that can be distributed

6. **What are the penalties for early withdrawal?**
   Know the costs of taking money from your retirement plan. Anything you take before age 59½ is taxed and has a 10 percent penalty associated with it. If you withdraw funds between the ages of 59½ and 70½, you will pay tax but no penalty. After age 70½, you are already required to take out your retirement funds.

(continued)

10 QUESTIONS TO ASK YOURSELF BEFORE WITHDRAWING RETIREMENT FUNDS

(continued from previous page)

7. **Are you changing jobs?**
   Some people may cash out their retirement plans from their employer when the leave a job rather than rolling the money over into an IRA or some other tax-deferred investment vehicle. Consider your options when leaving jobs. You may not even need that money, and some employers may let you keep it within their plans.

8. **How much can I withdraw?**
   Generally, you can't take out more money than the total amount you've put into the plan. All plans are different and have different rules. Check with your employer.

9. **Can I withdraw my employer's contributions?**
   Some employers provide contributions or a match to your contributions. It is an incentive to be in the plan and is often a benefit to you as an employee of the company. Sometimes, depending on your employer's policy, those extra contributions are available to be withdrawn. This is the case when the funds are vested or once the company deems that you own the funds. Each company has different vesting periods, and you will need to check with your employer.

10. **Have you consulted a professional?**
    Financial decisions such as prematurely taking money from your retirement fund should not be made lightly. Future income might be affected, and tax penalties will be incurred. Talk to a professional about your options before and after the withdrawal to ensure you are making the right choice with the right plan in place.

Issues to Consider When Withdrawing Funds

The biggest take-home message in this step of the book is that withdrawals from retirement funds should only occur at the appropriate times (i.e., avoid early withdrawal). That said, the government requires that you begin taking your employer-sponsored funds at age 70½ whether you are ready or not. What is the best way to withdraw your funds?

Retirement experts have identified several issues you need to consider before you withdraw your money: time horizon, asset allocation, and investment return volatility.

Time Horizon

The earlier you begin withdrawal, the lower your annual percentage will be if you want your savings to last. Why? Let's assume you live 20 to 30 years (or more) beyond retirement. And let's also assume you start taking money at age 63. Some experts believe it is wiser to take only 2 to 3 percent of your earnings per year if you want it to last. By contrast, if you start withdrawing money at age 70, you would be able to take a higher percentage of 6 or 7 percent each year because you started withdrawing later.

Asset Allocation

Your asset allocation mix will also determine how much you can safely withdraw from your accounts. The higher your percentage in stocks, the more you can withdraw. If you become too conservative as you get older and try too hard to maintain your assets, you may have invested in "safer" bond-type funds. As a result, you would need to withdraw smaller amounts because the returns over a longer period of time would not meet those of stock portfolios.

Investment Return Volatility

How much you earn also determines how much you can withdraw. The first two years of retirement are critical. If you incur losses, the ability to catch up becomes more difficult. Let's say you have $300,000 in your retirement savings account and would like to withdraw 4 percent per year for 30 years. If your investments decline by 10 percent in the first year of retirement, you are down to $258,000, including your withdrawals. You will need to reduce future withdrawals and attempt to catch up to make up the difference later.

What, When, How, and Why

You've shored up your funds and considered your time horizons. Now, it's time to look at the strategy at divestiture and the best order for withdrawal. If you could, you should try to live off of dividends and interest that your retirement savings plan pays. Unfortunately, this is only possible for people with very large portfolios.

WITHDRAWAL: WHICH OPTION TO CHOOSE?

John is a 72-year-old retiree who is in a 25 percent tax bracket and wants to take $18,000 out of a traditional IRA. He will pay $4,500 in taxes from the withdrawal. However, if he decides to take the same amount from a Roth IRA (an IRA in which withdrawals are not taxed and there is no minimum distribution), he won't have to pay any tax. If there is no required minimum distribution from a Roth IRA and John decides not to withdraw the money from that plan, he could, for example, earn 5 percent per year for another 10 years, in which case the original $18,000 would increase to $29,320. Not only that, but these additional earnings would be tax-free at the time he does decide to withdraw from the Roth IRA. So, the taxable traditional IRA would be the better option for withdrawal.

Conventional and expert wisdom will tell you to take money from taxable accounts first, such as bank accounts, traditional IRAs, and other savings accounts.

Selling your investments in taxable accounts first makes the most sense because tax-deferred accounts would be taxed as ordinary income—generally, a higher tax rate. Taking from your IRA before a regular account also means losing compounding growth over time.

Once a year, it is also a good idea to rebalance your portfolio to make sure you are sticking with your strategy. If you have a 60 percent stock and 40 percent bond split and this goes out of alignment, you can cash out some investments to get the portfolio back on track. Brokerage firm Charles Schwab suggests selling your investments with the poorest ratings first.

Once you have exhausted these options, you would withdraw from your tax-deferred plans or 401(k). First, you would look to your traditional IRA (see the sidebar), then your 401(k) plan, and lastly your Roth IRA.

This is probably a good time to revisit your numbers. In other words, as you consider your withdrawal strategy, you will have to know how much you can live on, what it will take to satisfy your lifestyle, and if your investments (even after retirement) are paying the kinds of returns you need to survive. Just because you are into retirement, withdrawing money can have many of the same investment issues as when you were saving. Rebalancing, understanding inflation and how it affects your savings, and understanding what your needs are (and will be) should still be part of your strategy for the rest of your life.

It's also important to remember that nothing is set in stone. Just because you've settled on a withdrawal rate and strategy today doesn't mean it can't or shouldn't change tomorrow. Yearly rebalances and discussions with an advisor are a good idea. Also, if you don't need the money, don't take it out. Give yourself some breathing room if you are not using the funds this year.

Some advisors also recommend a cash balance to cover 12 months of living expenses, as well as annuities that provide guaranteed income streams. These are predictable and will help you with your planning. They can also help combat healthcare and other nursing-related costs in the future. Overall, preparation and continual monitoring is key. Even if you are doing everything "right" and have worked your way through taxable accounts first and then into tax-deferred accounts, your job is to make sure you are acting defensively against down markets and inflation when necessary. Try not to get complacent in retirement.

Borrowing From Your 401(k)

According to the Employee Benefit Research Institute, 21 percent of all 401(k) participants who were eligible for loans had taken out loans from their plans.

Nearly 95 percent of plans have a loan provision. Most of them offer general-purpose loans that allow participants to borrow money for any reason as long as it is paid back in five years. According to a 2011 report from the consulting firm Aon Hewitt, more than three-quarters of plans allow participants to take loans for the purpose of buying a home with an extended repayment period, often between 10 and 30 years. Also, the same report found that 58 percent of plans allow their participants to have two or more loans at any one time. The age range with the highest percentage of loans is 40 to 49 years, with more than 32 percent of people in the range taking loans.

According to the report, the good news is that more than 81 percent of participants with a loan continued to defer money toward their DC or 401(k) plans. However, the savings rate was lower for those who had loans than those who did not have loans.

When It Makes Sense

It's never really a great idea to borrow from your 401(k) for a host of reasons, but there are some positives to the transaction if you do need the money.

Ease

Generally, getting a 401(k) loan is relatively easy without a lengthy process and without credit checks. Many companies allow you to do it through their websites, and it will not generate any credit inquiries. If you absolutely need the money quickly, you can have that convenience.

Payment

Unlike a mortgage or car loan, many 401(k) loans do not have a penalty if you pay off your loan faster than the five-year term. This can often be done through payroll deductions.

Cost

There are no costs associated with taking money from your own 401(k) plan. Investments that you have specified are liquidated, allowing you to borrow that money. Because of this, it is often better to take a loan when you feel or know the markets are weak. This way you are not negatively affected by the downside losses by having divested some of your funds.

Why Not to Borrow

If you've ever been on a diet, you know that it's hard to make a list of foods you shouldn't be eating. The same is true when you are looking to get money you need or want. You know you shouldn't borrow money, but you might borrow it anyway. Here are some reasons not to borrow your own money:

1. **Stating the obvious, you are borrowing and not saving.** Two things are occurring at this point. You have stopped contributing to your retirement plan, and the money you would have contributed is not making any money for you. Some plans don't allow you to contribute if you have an outstanding loan. Even if they do, it can sometimes be difficult to do both.

2. **You are losing money.** When you borrow from your 401(k) plan, a few things are happening. Contributions are not being made, and you will have to pay yourself back with interest. That rate is generally so low it can never come close to catching up to the returns you might have earned if the money stayed in the fund. Also, the money you are paying yourself back with is after-tax money. For example, if you earn one dollar but you are in a 25 percent tax bracket, your earnings really only give you 75 cents toward repaying the loan, and the 75 cents will be taxed when you withdraw the money from your retirement plan after retirement. Taxes will hurt you in both cases.

3. **Time has been lost.** Over time, your portfolio is unlikely to reach the levels it would have if you not borrowed money from your retirement savings plan. A home purchase, for example, would be a loss on the opportunity to grow money and likely not provide you an opportunity to make up for lost time.

4. **What if you lose your job or your financial situation gets worse?** Unpaid loans are considered a withdrawal and will be subject to taxes and penalties.

5. **Your cushion starts to disappear.** As stated earlier, using retirement money for other purposes and using it before retirement is basically a no-no. Taking the money for frivolous reasons diminishes your savings and hinders you from having it when you really need it.

6. **Consider your spending habits.** Are you buying things you can't afford with your borrowed retirement money? Reevaluate and see if you really need what you are borrowing the money for and if you should change your spending habits rather than deplete your savings.

7. **You are stuck in golden handcuffs.** If you quit your job, most plans expect repayment of your loan immediately. If you can't manage that but are unhappy in your present situation, you might be stuck for a while as you continue to pay down the debt.

8. **It's the opposite of paying yourself first.** Borrowing is not saving. If you recall from earlier in this book, one of the best ways to start your retirement savings journey is to always pay yourself first.

9. **There are fees associated with the loans.** Some companies will charge their employees for borrowing funds from their retirement plans. Do you really want to add insult to injury and add fees to the interest and lack of revenue you are already incurring?

10. **Your take-home pay is affected.** Loan repayments come out of your paycheck, so you will see your actual take-home pay lowered until you pay back the money. If budgeting is a problem, this could prevent you from paying your monthly bills. It's a slippery slope to debt and bankruptcy.

It's generally agreed that borrowing from your retirement plan should only be done in dire emergencies. Even a down payment for a home and college tuition should be sought elsewhere for the very reasons stated above. The government and your employer do provide hardship reasons for borrowing, but if you can avoid it, look elsewhere for the money or revisit your needs.

The "4 Percent" Rule

Let's say you've made it this far with a healthy retirement balance. You've saved $500,000, you avoided borrowing from your plan, and now it's time to consider how much to withdraw from your plan in order to maintain your lifestyle and live comfortably. Earlier in the book, there were several examples of people who wanted to take 4 percent per year for their incomes. The number four is not coincidental.

William Bengen, a financial services expert in California, came up with the "4 percent" rule in 1993. The rule states that if you take out 4.5 percent (not the actual "four" that the name suggests) of your savings each year (generally a portfolio with a 60 percent stock and 40 percent fixed-income split), your savings would last about 30 years, which is the time usually used for calculating retirement savings. Unfortunately, when that calculation was made, most portfolios were earning about 8 percent per year.

Portfolios these days earn much less—in some cases, half—and the 4 percent rule is being debunked.

A report from investment firm J.P. Morgan found that you may want to consider a "portfolio-based solution" rather than outdated rules that do not reflect the current economic environment. The J.P. Morgan method recali-brates withdrawal rates and asset allocation each year. This does two things: (1) recognizes changes in your financial situation from year to year and (2) recognizes that markets are dynamic and also change from year to year. J.P. Morgan also says that as you retire, you may want to rethink your asset-allo-cation strategy over time. As you get older, you should consider decreasing your exposure to equity-type investments.

The truth is that each investor is different and has unique circumstances. Consider the following:

- Taxes are generally not part of the 4 percent rule equation. You will need to factor that in.

- Taking 4 percent of your income may be more than you need and cause you to use up funds prematurely.

- Alternatively, 4 percent may be too little to meet your needs.

- Expenses are not stagnant and change from year to year.

- Thirty years of withdrawals might be too much or too little. The cal-culations will not work for everyone.

Like any part of your retirement plan, keeping an open mind and staying as flexible as possible is the best option. The 4 percent rule is a guideline that can work but, again, was created at a time when interest rates and port-folios were expected to earn much more than they do today.

Discussing your options with your advisor, rebalancing and recalibrat-ing your portfolio, and looking at other options such as annuities and the percentages you do intend to withdraw should all be part of your plan going forward. Also, consider your spending habits in up-market cycles versus down-market cycles. If you need to readjust your spending, do so, because it will help you better gauge your withdrawal needs. In other words, expect the unexpected and plan accordingly. Do not rely on one method to answer all your needs.

As we continue with the discussion, we will start to look at how health-care costs and Social Security play into assessing your financial needs.

STEP

GET THE MOST OUT OF
SOCIAL SECURITY

In step 2, the concept of the "three-legged stool" of retirement was discussed. You will recall that retirement savings should be made of three parts, hence the three legs. Private savings represents one leg, employer-sponsored plans represent the second leg, and Social Security represents the third and final leg on which the entire stool, or your retirement plan, is supported.

Also in step 2, we mentioned that according to an Employee Benefit Research Institute report, Social Security for people 65 and older accounts for 40 percent of their income.

What Exactly Is Social Security?

In 1935, President Franklin Delano Roosevelt signed the Social Security Act into law as part of his New Deal policies, which he put into motion at the height of the Great Depression. When it was enacted, it was meant as a retirement-only benefit for workers. A law in 1939 amended it to include survivor benefits for children and spouses of retirees. Today, disabled workers and their families can also receive Social Security.

The system is "pay-as-you-go," which means people working today are paying for current retiree benefits. There is no build-up of assets like a DB plan. This is somewhat problematic as the demographics shift to an older population, and fewer people are paying in for a larger number of Americans. It is for this reason that many people younger than 55 years believe Social Security may not be there when it is their time to withdraw from it. However, raising the age of full eligibility from 65 to 67 and enacted benefit reductions are helping with this issue. During the George W. Bush presidency, there was some debate about privatization and giving people investment freedom when it comes to their own Social Security funding. That debate never really got very far and will not be addressed in this book.

How Does (How Should) Social Security Work Within Your Retirement Plan?

According to the Social Security Administration (SSA), Social Security will account for only about 40 percent of your income. This underscores why you will want to ensure that you take advantage of all savings opportunities.

Planning is important when considering how Social Security will work within your retirement plans. Taking benefits at **full retirement age (FRA)** is called the **primary insurance amount**. Full retirement age will vary depending on your year of birth. When Social Security was first created, FRA was 65 years old. Today it is 67, as shown in the following chart.

Year Born	FRA
1937 or earlier	65
1938–1942	65 + 2 months for every year after 1937
1943–1954	66
1955–1959	66 + 2 months for every year after 1954
1960+	67

To determine your primary insurance amount, the SSA takes your best 35 years of employment to reach something called **average indexed monthly earnings**. Social Security is also indexed for inflation or **cost-of-living adjustments**.

The SSA provides several calculators to estimate how much you will receive (see Resources, page 134). The amount you receive depends on the specific information you provide.

The age at which you decide to take Social Security will affect how you determine your withdrawal rates and future required income. As you approach retirement, it's best to get a sense of what path you might take. Taking benefits at age 62 will reduce the amount of Social Security you receive, and waiting until FRA will increase the amount you get. This is an important variable in your retirement income decisions.

Collecting benefits before you reach your FRA will subject you to earnings tests every year until you reach full retirement. If your earnings are higher than the SSA's limits, benefits will be withheld. This is another calculation you need to consider when determining all your savings (private and government) at the time of your retirement.

Benefits that are held back by the SSA are not refunded. However, if your FRA is 66 years old, for example, and you starting taking funds at 62, the SSA would have taken 25 percent of your benefits. If you returned to work at age 64, you may have had two years of benefits withheld by the time you reach full retirement age. So, the 25 percent reduction would be decreased and you would receive credit for the two years you lost Social Security. Your new benefits would be calculated as if you started withdrawing funds at age 64.

Once you've identified your Social Security benefits and you know if you will be working or drawing on other retirement funds, you need to figure out your living expenses. This was discussed in step 4 in relation to withdrawals from your account. So, you may already have some kind of estimate of your living expenses.

Again, keep in mind that Social Security is about 40 percent of your income. This, in combination with your other savings and expenses, should give you a pretty good picture of how the plans will all work together.

Charting Your Social Security Benefits

The SSA says deciding on how and when to start taking Social Security is a personal decision. Only you know your income needs, health, desire to work into retirement, amount of your other savings, and future obligations. As the following chart shows, taking payments earlier or later can have a significant impact on the amount of money you will receive in retirement.

The chart below shows, very clearly, the consequences of early retirement benefits. If your FRA is 66 years old, you would receive a benefit of $1,000 per month. However, if you choose to start receiving benefits at age 62, a 25 percent reduction is incurred on your benefits and you would receive only $750 per month. You receive those payments for a longer period of time or from an earlier age, but the reduction is permanent.

Alternatively, you could wait past your FRA and receive benefits at age 70, in which case your monthly benefit would rise to $1,320 per month.

Some considerations the SSA says you need to keep in mind when making that decision, are the following:

- Are you still working?
- Do you come from a family with good health?
- How is your own health?
- Will you still have health insurance?

ESTIMATE OF MONTHLY SOCIAL SECURITY BENEFITS

Monthly benefit amounts differ based on the age you decide to start receiving benefits. This example assumes a benefit of $1,000 at a full retirement age of 66.

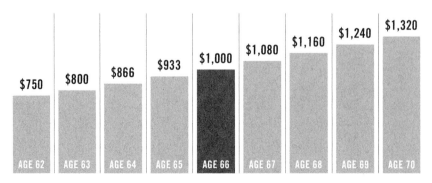

- Are you eligible for benefits on someone else's record?

- Do you have other income to support you if you decide to delay taking your benefits?

- Will other family members qualify for benefits with you on your record?

By using one of the calculators previously mentioned, you can estimate your benefits, life expectancy, and earnings limit.

The chart below shows an example of what earnings are withheld and how they are calculated if you take benefits when you are younger or older than your FRA.

People younger than FRA will lose one dollar of benefits for every two dollars they make above $15,720 per year. As you reach FRA, your benefit is reduced by one dollar for every three dollars earned above $41,880 prior to reaching FRA. Beyond FRA, there are no benefit penalties.

There are provisions if you change your mind. You can withdraw an early withdrawal application and reapply when you feel you are ready. So, you are not necessarily stuck with lower monthly payments if you don't want them. Assess your situation carefully, but as changes occur, you can switch directions as necessary.

2015 RETIREMENT EARNINGS LIMIT

Under FRA
- $1 of benefits withheld for every $2 in earnings above $15,720
- Earned $25,720 − $15,720 = $10,000 over × ½ = $5,000 withheld

---

Year individual reaches FRA
- $1 of benefits withheld for every $3 in earnings above $41,880 for months prior to attaining FRA
- Earned $51,880 − $41,880 = $10,000 over × ⅓ = $3,333 withheld

---

Month individual reaches FRA and beyond
- Unlimited

Survivor Benefits

The idea of death is obviously a hard subject for many of us to tackle. However, when it comes to retirement and Social Security, it should be something we make provisions for and are conscious about.

Social Security can be more than just a retirement savings vehicle. It also provides survivors insurance in case a worker dies. This is generally calculated by the amount of time a person has worked and the amount of money put into the plan.

Why is this significant? Besides any private health insurance you may have, the Social Security survivor benefits can help you assess your income streams if you prematurely die and leave your family without a primary breadwinner. It's an important part of your strategy and should not be taken for granted just because you think that it will never happen.

The following people can receive payments:

- Widow or widower (A widow or widower can take reduced benefits as early as 60 years or full benefits at FRA.)
- Unmarried children under the age of 18
- Dependent parents aged 62 and older
- Disabled people at age 50, if the disability started before or within seven years of your death

Much like your Social Security retirement benefits, your survivor benefits depend on your lifetime earnings. The more time you worked, the greater their benefits.

Social Security and Taxes

In general, 40 percent of people who receive Social Security benefits pay taxes on them.

An individual will pay taxes if he or she earns more than $25,000 a year.

Couples will pay taxes if they have a combined income of more than $32,000 a year.

Sound tax planning can help you when dealing with Social Security benefits. Once you know what your annual required minimum withdrawals will

SOCIAL SECURITY SPOUSAL PAYMENT EXAMPLE

Let's look at the case of George and Martha. Assuming they are both 62 years old, Martha would like to get her retirement benefit early. George decides to wait for full retirement and take his benefits at age 70. Between the ages of 62 and 66, Martha would be getting a reduced benefit. However, she is under no obligation to take her spousal benefit, which would be reduced, because George hasn't yet begun collecting anything.

When Martha turns 66 (her FRA), she can begin to collect a full spousal benefit because George has qualified her to do so by filing and suspending his retirement benefits.

However, Martha's unreduced spousal benefit is calculated as 50 percent of George's full retirement benefit minus Martha's full retirement benefit. She will then receive a total benefit equal to her own reduced retirement benefit plus her unreduced excess spousal benefit. This total is less than half of George's full retirement benefit.

be, you might be able to postpone or time-out other withdrawals (e.g., IRAs, other investments) so that your benefits are taxed only in alternate years.

Withdrawing tax-free savings from a Roth IRA can help put Social Security benefits in a tax-free area of your portfolio. Stock sales and other investments can be timed for sell-offs that work within your schedule. If you can manage to take some profit in years when 85 percent of your benefits will be taxed, you have a greater chance of limiting your gains and reducing the amount of your benefits that will be taxed.

Spousal Benefits

The SSA says that spouses are eligible to get a benefit "equal to one-half of your full retirement-benefit amount if they start receiving benefits at their full retirement age."

However, this is only the case if your spouse isn't getting benefits on his or her own from the SSA. If your spouse is collecting his or her own retirement benefit, then this benefit is calculated differently. The SSA calculates it as half of your full retirement benefit minus your spouse's full benefits.

Other Factors That Can Affect Social Security Benefits

Social Security, assuming you have paid into it, will be a retirement-savings vehicle that at least you know can be calculated within your overall strategy. However, there are factors that can affect—both positively and negatively— the benefits you receive.

- **Working and taking benefits:** It is perfectly legitimate to continue working while you are receiving your Social Security benefits. Because of the way the SSA calculates benefits, if you are earning more than one of the years they used to assess your benefit, an increase will be recalculated and more money will be paid out to you as part of your benefit.

- **Government Pension Offset:** Working for a government agency and receiving a pension from a federal, state, or local job you held where you did not pay into Social Security will affect your spouse or widow's pension. The Government Pension Offset will reduce the amount of your Social Security by two-thirds the amount of your government pension.

- **Being self-employed:** According to the SSA, there is a maximum amount of earnings for which you will pay Social Security taxes. For 2014, the maximum amount of taxable earnings was $117,000.

- **Social Security credits:** Credits are how the SSA calculates if you have worked enough to qualify for benefits. Credits will always stay on your record, whether you stop and start working again later or are working without any gaps in time. The SSA will not pay benefits if you do not have the right amount of credits.

You must earn $1,200 to get one Social Security or work credit and $4,800 to get the maximum four credits for the year. Earning extra credits will not increase your benefit amount.

GOVERNMENT PENSION OFFSET EXAMPLE

If you receive a government pension every month of $600, two-thirds of that, or $400, will be used to offset your Social Security spousal or widow's pension. So, if you are eligible to receive a $500 spousal benefit, you will only get back $100 per month ($500 government pension − $400 (two-thirds offset) = $100).

It may seem like a relatively simple part of your retirement planning, but Social Security, as we have just seen, has a great number of nuances and areas for reductions and increases. Social Security can affect your overall retirement strategy, depending on when you choose to take benefits. It's wise to look at Social Security as seriously as you would your own private investments to ensure your strategies complement one another. It's better to know ahead of time what you will be getting. Don't be surprised late in the game.

As we continue on our journey, we will discuss the role of taxes, a topic that has not come up too much yet. Taxes will be addressed in more detail in step 6. There are consequences of taxable investments, and they could make a big difference in your retirement savings.

STEP

GET THE MOST OUT OF TAXES

Taxes on your retirement income are almost guaranteed. However, the questions remain: How much tax will you pay, how much of a bite will it take out of your savings, and is there anything you can do to minimize the burden?

Let's start with this basic concept: All of the retirement savings plans and methods to store away money for your golden years are usually tax-deferred savings. By putting money into your 401(k), other employer-sponsored plans, and federally sanctioned personal plans such as IRAs, you have deferred taxes and potentially lowered them on the back end, but you have not avoided them completely.

With that in mind, it's important to know that the IRS considers withdrawals you make in retirement to be ordinary income. The general principle behind tax-deferral plans is that, in retirement, you would have reached a lower tax bracket than in your earning years and you will be taxed at lower rates.

However, this is not always the case. Large lump-sum withdrawals, combined pensions with your spouse, or the amounts you have saved up to this point may push you into a higher tax bracket than you are at now, which would be unfortunate. Also, you generally have fewer write-offs in retirement. If you've paid off your mortgage, that too is one less (large) deduction you will no longer be making. If you have less disposable income, you will be making fewer charitable donations than you currently do as well, for example.

Different Plans and Their Tax Implications

Roth IRAs

Roth IRAs serve as the one investment in this list that is not subject to being taxed when funds are withdrawn. Money going into the savings plan is taxed but earns revenue and can be withdrawn tax-free as long as you've had the account for at least five years and you have reached the age of 59 ½. Much like the traditional IRA, you can be penalized 10 percent if you choose to withdraw funds prior to reaching the age of 59 ½.

IRAs

As discussed in step 4, money taken out of an IRA before age 59 ½ is not only taxable but also usually comes with a 10 percent penalty. You don't want to be penalized twice.

Employer-Sponsored Plans

As mentioned previously, most employer-sponsored retirement plans are taxable when withdrawals begin, usually at whatever tax bracket you find yourself in at the time. Also, as discussed in step 4, required minimum distributions are necessary after April 1 of the year you turn 70 ½ years old.

Social Security

Social Security benefits are not taxed if it is your only source of income. If you receive income from other sources, your Social Security benefits may not be taxed unless your gross income is more than the "base amount."

Base amounts are:

- $32,000 for married couples filing jointly

- $25,000 for single, head of household, qualifying widow/widower with a dependent child, or married individuals filing separately who did not live with their spouses at any time during the year

- $0 for married people filing separately who lived together during the year

Some of you might be tempted to convert some or all of your employer-sponsored retirement savings or other IRA money into a Roth IRA to take advantage of tax-free withdrawals. Keep in mind that the other withdrawals you intend to roll over will be taxed at your normal income levels and could push you into higher brackets depending on the lump sum you take out. In those cases, it might be better to spread the withdrawals over time or at least discuss your options with your financial planner and/or accountant.

How Taxes Work in Retirement

Let's say that Dick and Jane, a retired couple in their 60s, are each receiving some form of pension. Dick is getting $2,200 per month from Social Security, and Jane gets $785 per month from Social Security.

Dick has a company pension plan as well, and he receives $1,100 per month from that. He also has an IRA worth $150,000. His wife, Jane, is getting $7,000 per year from an at-home job and has a Roth IRA worth $40,000. They also have traditional savings of $10,000 in a joint savings account.

It's likely that Dick and Jane will pay little or no taxes. Why?

The combined pensions and income do not meet the threshold to make Social Security benefits subject to tax. Deductions, in this case, will probably be more than the income they report. When Dick is subject to required minimum distributions from his IRA, he may find his income will be higher than the Social Security benchmark. However, it is not a certainty. Even in that case, the taxes may likely be minimal.

Everyone's scenario is different. Your pensions, savings, income, and Social Security, along with that of your spouse, will vary from person to person. This is when taxes become important, and your planning for taxes in retirement also becomes important. Just as you've been looking at the right savings plans and investments to maximize your retirement savings, preparing for expenses (in this case, your taxes) will be equally as important. Again, large lump-sum withdrawals and incomes that are above Social Security benchmarks can put you in a high tax bracket and, in some cases, higher than when you were working. Don't get caught off guard. Make sure you know what your monthly income/withdrawals will be when you are preparing for this part of retirement expenses. Later in this step, we will discuss how to select the right professional help to navigate these issues and some of the questions you should ask.

The IRS has created the following worksheet that helps you determine your minimum required distributions from your IRA:

1. IRA balance on December 31 of the previous year.   _____

2. Distribution period from the table below for your age on your birthday this year.   _____

3. Line 1 divided by number entered on line 2 = your RMD for this year for this IRA. _____

4. Repeat Steps 1 through 3 for each of your IRAs.

(Once you determine a separate RMD from each of your traditional IRAs, you can total these minimum amounts and take them from any one or more of your traditional IRAs.)

Age	Distrib. Period	Age	Distrib. Period	Age	Distrib. Period	Age	Distrib. Period	Age	Distrib. Period
70	27.4	80	18.7	90	11.4	100	6.3	110	3.1
71	26.5	81	17.9	91	10.8	101	5.9	111	2.9
72	25.6	82	17.1	92	10.2	102	5.5	112	2.6
73	24.7	83	16.3	93	9.6	103	5.2	113	2.4
74	23.8	84	15.5	94	9.1	104	4.9	114	2.1
75	22.9	85	14.8	95	8.6	105	4.5	115+	1.9
76	22.0	86	14.1	96	8.1	106	4.2		
77	21.2	87	13.4	97	7.6	107	3.9		
78	20.3	88	12.7	98	7.1	108	3.7		
79	19.5	89	12.0	99	6.7	109	3.4		

Taxable Investments

Having earned savings within tax-deferred retirement vehicles, many of your investments are taxable. As we have discussed, all withdrawals are taxable at regular income levels.

Stocks/Mutual Funds

Holding stocks outside of a 401(k) or other retirement savings can cost you tax on dividends if your stock pays them, as well as profit or capital gains you make on the investment. However, capital gains and dividends are not taxed if they are held within a tax-deferred account, and won't be until they are removed or sold from the account.

Bonds and Bond Funds

Bonds and bond funds are taxed similarly to stocks in that while they are held within a tax-deferred account, they will not incur any tax.

Just as capital gains can increase your tax burden, a capital loss can help offset your income. You can use your capital losses from one investment to decrease the capital gains from another. Also, capital losses not used this year can offset future capital gains.

Municipal Bonds and Treasuries

Most federal and state bonds are tax-exempt depending on the type of investment you are making.

Annuities

A so-called qualified annuity (401(k) and other retirement plans are qualified investment vehicles) is taxed the same as other tax-deferred plans when withdrawals begin. For nonqualified annuities, the tax rule on withdrawals is "interest and earnings first."

Under this rule, interest and earnings are considered withdrawn first for federal income tax purposes. For example, if you invested $25,000 in a fixed or variable annuity and it is now worth $45,000, you would be taxed on the first $20,000 you withdraw. The remaining $25,000 is considered a return of principal, and you would not be taxed on it. Withdrawals are taxed until all interest and earnings have been taken out, at which point the principal can be withdrawn without any tax penalty to you.

TABLE 6.1: CALCULATING TAXABLE BENEFITS

Income	Brad	Angelina
Pension received	$22,000	$0
Interest earned	$500	$0
½ Social Security	$3,750	$1,750
Total	$26,250	$1,750

Brad and Angelina's provisional income = $28,000

Consider the calculating taxable benefits example. Brad receives a taxable pension of $22,000 and interest of $500. His annual Social Security is $7,500 (half is shown in the chart for calculation purposes). Angelina receives only $3,500 of Social Security (again, half is being used in calculation). Their total provisional income (pension + interest + half of each other's Social Security benefits) is $28,000.

Their combined income is below $32,000, so they would not be taxed if they were filing jointly. For a single taxpayer, the threshold is $25,000.

You can quickly calculate your taxable benefits using the following worksheet:

Start with 50% of Social Security benefits received	$_____
Add additional income	$_____
Total equals combined income	$_____

The following are other worksheets that can help you (whether you are married or single) determine your taxable benefits and if they've passed the income limit for which you will have to pay taxes on Social Security.

CALCULATING TAXABLE BENEFITS

SINGLE PEOPLE WITH INCOME BETWEEN $25,000 AND $34,000

1. Start with **50%** of your total annual SS benefit

2. Enter the sum of your additional wages for the year   +

3. Add the two together to arrive at Total Combined Income   =
(Must be between $25,000–$34,000)

4. Subtract **$25,000**   − **$25,000**

   Difference   =

5. Multiply by **50%**   × **0.50**

   Total   =

6. Compare **Total** to **50%** of SS benefit (Line 1).
The amount of your Social Security benefits
subject to taxes is the lesser of the two items.

MARRIED PEOPLE WITH INCOME BETWEEN $25,000 AND $34,000

1. Start with **50%** of your total annual SS benefit

2. Enter the sum of your additional wages for the year   +

3. Add the two together to arrive at Total Combined Income   =
(Must be between $32,000–$44,000)

4. Subtract **$32,000**   − **$32,000**

   Difference   =

5. Multiply by **50%**   × **0.50**

   Total   =

6. Compare **Total** to **50%** of SS benefit (Line 1).
The amount of your Social Security benefits
subject to taxes is the lesser of the two items.

SOURCE: AARP

SINGLE PEOPLE WITH INCOME BETWEEN $25,000 AND $34,000

1. Start with **50%** of your total annual SS benefit ....

2. Enter the sum of your additional wages for the year .... +

3. Add the two together to arrive at Total Combined Income .... =
(Must be greater than $34,000)

4. Subtract **$34,000** .... −   **$34,000**

Difference .... =

5. Multiply by **85%** .... ×   **0.85**

Total .... =

6. Calculate three possible options and choose the smallest

OPTION A

Start with the Base Amount (Line 5) ....

Add **$4,500** .... +   **$4,500**

Option A Total .... =

OPTION B

Start with Total Combined Income (Line 3) ....

Subtract **$25,000** .... −   **$25,000**

Subtotal .... =

Multiply by **50%** .... ×   **0.50**

Option B Total .... =

OPTION C

Start with total Social Security Benefits ....

Multiply by **85%** to arrive at the .... ×   **0.85**

Option C Total .... =

Compare the **Totals** from **Options A, B,** and **C**.
Your Social Security benefits subject to taxes is
the lesser of the three options ....

SOURCE: AARP

MARRIED PEOPLE WITH INCOME BETWEEN $25,000 AND $34,000

1. Start with **50%** of your total annual SS benefit ....

2. Enter the sum of your additional wages for the year .... +

3. Add the two together to arrive at Total Combined Income .... =
(Must be greater than $44,000)

4. Subtract **$44,000** .... − $44,000

Difference .... =

5. Multiply by **85%** .... ×   0.85

Total .... =

6. Calculate three possible options and choose the smallest

OPTION A

Start with the Base Amount (Line 5) ....

Add **$6,000** .... + $6,000

Option A Total .... =

OPTION B

Start with Total Combined Income (Line 3) ....

Subtract **$32,000** .... − $32,000

Subtotal .... =

Multiply by **50%** .... ×   0.50

Option B Total .... =

OPTION C

Start with total Social Security Benefits ....

Multiply by **85%** to arrive at the .... ×   0.85

Option C Total .... =

Compare the **Totals** from **Options A, B,** and **C**.
Your Social Security benefits subject to taxes is
the lesser of the three options ....

SOURCE: AARP

TOP 10 WAYS TO REDUCE YOUR TAX BURDEN

You can't avoid the inevitable, but you can make it a little easier to digest. Here are some ways to lighten your tax burden in retirement and hold on to as much of your hard-earned savings as possible.

1. **Take advantage of Roth IRAs.** You can help curb the tax load and take money out tax-free (as long as you are the right age) because you are paying the tax when you contribute and not when you withdraw. However, you want to contribute and pay tax at your lowest possible rates to get the most benefit from it.

2. **Use capital losses.** As mentioned earlier in this step, capital losses on one investment can be used to offset gains from another. Make sure your planner or advisor is keeping track and ensuring the best possible tax outcomes.

3. **Delay withdrawals on 401(k) plans.** If you choose to work or need to work beyond age 70, many plans will allow you to defer distribution on your 401(k) plans until you retire completely.

4. **Time your withdrawals properly.** Retirees with more than one savings account will want to time out their withdrawals. Lump-sum withdrawals or large amounts will cause negative tax implications. If you time it properly and plan accordingly, you can withdraw what you need without incurring too much tax.

5. **Move locations.** Many of you might consider retirement as a chance to move to a warmer location or be closer to your grandkids. There are states that have less tax or no tax, and moving to one of them is an option that can reduce your tax burden.

6. **Give it away.** If you are considering giving some of your income away to kids or charity, the IRS now allows annual tax-free gifts (cash or other assets) up to $14,000 per year.

7. **Withdraw properly.** We have discussed why you should take withdrawals from taxable accounts first. You can benefit from low capital gains rates while investments in your tax-deferred and tax-free retirement accounts continue to grow.

8. **Diversify.** By having more than one retirement savings account, you give yourself diversity and the flexibility to make choices upon your retirement. All your eggs in one basket will limit your options, and you may find you can't exercise the best tax advantages when you retire.

9. **Move assets to your spouse.** If your spouse does not pay taxes or is in a lower tax bracket than you, it could be worth transferring income-producing assets into his or her name. This could reduce your income to below the level at which your personal allowances start to be withdrawn.

10. **Postpone income.** If, through proper planning, you think you will be in a lower tax bracket in one year compared with the previous one, postpone withdrawing income until that time to reduce your tax burden until you move into the lower tax bracket the following year.

TABLE 6.2: SPLITTING RETIREMENT ACCOUNTS TO REDUCE YOUR TAX BURDEN	
Taxable 401(k) or IRA	50/50 Split Roth IRA and taxable accounts
Required withdrawal at age 71: $37,736	Required withdrawal at age 71: $18,868
Potential tax bracket: 25%	Potential tax bracket: 15%
Note: Based on $1 million saved.	

SOURCE: Adapted from AARP.

How to Choose an Accountant

In step 3 you learned how to select the right financial advisor for your retirement needs. In this step, we provide tips on finding the right accountant for your retirement tax needs. The ideas and methods are similar to selecting a financial advisor because some of the information an accountant provides will help you maximize returns and reduce costs.

- **Start with referrals.** Much like the advisor selection, you can ask people your age who they might be thinking about using. Maybe they already know a tax accountant who can help you better plan your retirement and keep your taxes to a minimum.

- **The accountant's experience is important.** You want to ensure your accountant has experience in tax matters to help you navigate the tax minefield properly, as opposed to a small business accountant or someone who specializes in other things. A Certified Public Accountant (CPA) versus a non-CPA is something to consider. CPAs have the designation for a reason. They have more training, experience, and education than non-CPAs and might be the right fit for your needs.

- **Consider accountant fees.** Different accountants will charge different fees based on their experience or the firm for which they work. You will need to balance the amount you are paying to your accountant versus the potential savings provided and make sure you end up on the better end of that deal. Fees could also change depending on the complexities of your finances. Lower fees for easier returns and higher fees for more complex returns are possible.

- **Understand tax preparation versus tax planning.** Determine your needs first. If it is planning you need, choose an accountant with more skills and advisory tools at his or her disposal. A tax preparer will get your papers in order and prepare them but will have little to no skills in helping you plan for your future.

- **Consider your own income.** The more money you have and make, the more likely you will need an accountant for retirement. Consider choosing an accountant who is comfortable with high–net worth clients and able to manage your funds with the proper attention.

Moving ahead, we will begin looking at health-related expenses and issues that can affect you and your retirement savings.

10 QUESTIONS TO ASK YOUR ACCOUNTANT

1. **What is your experience?** Get to know your accountant's background like you would if you were hiring anyone else. You wouldn't hire someone to fix your bathroom sink who hadn't fixed one before.

2. **What are your designations?** Find out if the accountant is a tax preparer or tax planner. What are his or her qualifications?

3. **Do you work well with financial planners?** Make sure your accountant has the ability to work with any other people you might have looking after your funds. Sometimes there can be territorial issues, and you need everyone on your side with your best interests at heart.

4. **Can I talk to some of your other clients?** If an accountant is good at what he or she does, he or she should have clients you can chat with about their experiences.

5. **What are your fees?** How do they break down? Make sure you have a clear understanding of how the accountant charges fees and when and where other charges are tacked on.

6. **What is your availability?** What you don't want is to run into an accountant who only works around April 1. You need someone all year, at any time. Make sure your accountant is accessible.

7. **How often will we communicate?** Much like accessibility, you want an accountant to whom you can talk or who talks to you when changes and needs arise.

8. **Who will be doing the work?** If you are working with larger firms, the person you make initial contact with is often not the person handling the day-to-day work. Find out who handles your taxes and if that person is right for you.

9. **Are you proactive?** Will your accountant remind you of upcoming tax events, withdrawals, and payments, or will you be relied on to provide this information to your accountant? Judge your own needs and find the accountant that suits your character best.

10. **Why should I hire you?** It seems like a basic question, but the response you get might help you make a quick decision about the person sitting across from you. See if he or she is interested in your personal finances or are making more broad sweeping statements about taxes. The picture will become clear enough.

GET THE MOST OUT OF MEDICARE

We have often mentioned the need for you to understand your expenses in retirement. The better you can assess your expenses, the better you can plan your withdrawals, your income, and what shape your retirement lifestyle might take. Of course, there are no guarantees, and expenses will change from year to year.

Steps 7 and 8 will look at issues of healthcare and healthcare costs and how these expenses play into your planning and ultimate living requirements into retirement.

Medicare

What exactly is Medicare, and who can apply for it?

Nearly half a century ago, President Lyndon Johnson signed the Medicare bill into law. At its core, it is a federal health insurance program that pays for hospital and medical care for the elderly and certain disabled Americans. It has helped many people with high medical expenses at difficult times. Today, about 50 million people are covered by Medicare.

The Centers for Medicare and Medicaid Services, a branch of the US Department of Health and Human Services, is the federal agency that runs the Medicare program and monitors **Medicaid** programs offered by each state. It is funded through payroll taxes and other sources such as income taxes paid on Social Security benefits, certain kinds of interest, and premiums from people who aren't eligible for the premium-free part of the program.

Medicare and Retirement

The older you get, the more likely it is you will be spending money on healthcare-related issues and medications. Despite programs for the elderly, such as Medicare, there are still costs associated with healthcare, and you will still need to factor those costs into your retirement-planning expenses and savings. Contrary to what you might think, Medicare is not a free social program. Participants have to "pay to play."

There are four elements to Medicare that will be discussed in greater detail in this step:

1. **Medicare Part A,** which covers hospital costs

2. **Medicare Part B,** which covers doctor visits and outpatient treatments

3. **Medicare Part C,** which includes Parts A and B and is run by Medicare-approved private insurance providers

4. **Medicare Part D,** which covers a large number of prescription medications

Part A is prepaid by most of us through payroll taxes, but Part B and Part D are not. Subscribers pay premiums priced on a sliding scale that is based on income in retirement.

According to Fidelity Benefits Consulting, a 65-year-old couple retiring this year will need an average of $220,000 to cover medical expenses throughout their retirement.

It is important to note that the average cost people pay per year for Part B premiums is about $1,280 per year. So, as you factor in lifestyle, living expenses, and any other luxuries into your retirement funds, healthcare and Medicare expenses need to be considered as well.

RETIRING EARLY

Let's address the need for healthcare if you retire but you are younger than the Medicare-eligible age of 65. There are a few options available to you.

- You could become part of a younger spouse's health plan through his or her employer.
- You could get COBRA (Consolidated Omnibus Budget Reconciliation Act) coverage, which employers offer for up to 18 months after leaving the workplace.
- You could buy private health insurance as an interim measure.

How Do Medicare Benefits Work?

There are four elements to Medicare benefits.

1. **Medicare Part A: Hospital insurance**

   - Covers inpatient care in hospitals

   - Covers skilled nursing-facility care

   - Includes hospice care and home healthcare

2. **Medicare Part B: Medical insurance**

   - Covers services from doctors and other healthcare providers

   - Includes outpatient care and home healthcare

   - Covers durable medical equipment and some preventative services

3. **Medicare Part C: Medicare Advantage**

   - Includes all benefits and services covered under Part A and B

   - Features, usually, Medicare prescription drug coverage (Part D) as part of the plan

   - Is run by Medicare-approved private insurance companies

   - May include extra benefits and services for extra costs

4. **Medicare Part D: Medicare Prescription Drug Coverage**

- Helps with the cost of prescription drugs

- Is run by Medicare-approved private insurance companies

- May help lower your prescription drug costs and help protect against higher costs in the future

Each part represents different coverage and potentially different costs depending on what you require. Also, there are premiums associated with greater coverage and enrollment timeframes, which also depend on which service you select.

Medicare Costs

According to the Medicare.gov website, the following is what you can expect to pay for the different parts of the Medicare program:

- **Part A.** Most people don't pay a premium. If you need to buy it, it will cost up to $426.00 per month.

- **Part B.** Most people pay $104.90 per month. The Part B deductible is $147 per month.

- **Part C.** Varies by plan

- **Part D.** Varies by plan, but the cost goes up the higher your income

When you are thinking about Medicare for the first time or if you are interested in changing your coverage, the following items should be taken into consideration:

- **Convenience:** Where are your doctors located, and what are their hours? Do they keep electronic records and prescribe medication electronically? Which pharmacies do they use?

- **Coverage:** How well does the plan I am considering cover my needs?

- **Quality of care:** Services can vary, so you should assess your satisfaction with your medical care. Medicare often provides information to help you compare plans and providers.

- **Travel:** What coverage will you get if you move to another state or country?

COMPARE MEDICARE COVERAGE OPTIONS

There are two basic options for those who wish to enroll in a Medicare coverage plan: Original Medicare, and Medicare Advantage Plan. Use this comparative table to help you decide which Medicare coverage plan is right for you.

Original Medicare	Medicare Advantage Plan

KEY FEATURES OF BASIC COVERAGE

- Includes Part A , Hospital Insurance, and/or Part B, Medical Insurance.
- Medicare provides this coverage directly.
- You have your choice of doctors, hospitals, and other providers that accept Medicare.
- Generally, you or your supplemental coverage pay deductibles and coinsurance.
- You usually pay a monthly premium for Part B.

- Like an HMO or PPO.
- Part C includes both Part A, Hospital Insurance, & Part B, Medical Insurance.
- Private insurance companies approved by Medicare provide this coverage.
- In most plans, you need to use plan doctors, hospitals, and other providers or you may pay more or all of the costs.
- You may pay a monthly premium (in addition to your Part B premium) and a copayment or coinsurance for covered services.
- Costs, extra coverage, & rules vary by plan.

PRESCRIPTION DRUG COVERAGE OPTION

- If you want drug coverage, you must join a Medicare Prescription Drug Plan. You usually pay a monthly premium.
- These plans are run by private companies approved by Medicare.

- If you want drug coverage, and it's offered by your Medicare Advantage Plan, in most cases, you must get it through your plan.
- In some types of plans that don't offer drug coverage, you can join a Medicare Prescription Drug Plan.

SUPPLEMENTAL COVERAGE OPTION

- You may want to get coverage that fills gaps in Original Medicare coverage. You can choose to buy a Medicare Supplement Insurance (Medigap) policy from a private company.
- Costs vary by policy and company.
- Employers/unions may offer similar coverage.

If you join a Medicare Advantage Plan, you can't use Medicare Supplement Insurance (Medigap) to pay for out-of-pocket costs you have in the Medicare Advantage Plan.

If you already have a Medicare Advantage Plan, you can't be sold a Medigap policy.

You can only use a Medigap policy if you disenroll from your Medicare Advantage Plan and return to Original Medicare.

SOURCE: Adapted from www.medicare.gov.

- **Doctor choice:** Do your doctors accept the coverage you have? Do the doctors you want (in your network) accept new patients?

- **Prescription drugs:** Are you covered under a plan, or do you need to join a Medicare drug plan?

- **Other coverage:** Are you eligible for other health-related coverage? If so, find out how or if the coverage works with Medicare.

How and Why to Enroll in Medicare

Medicare enrollment can be a bit of a maze if it is not done properly or you are making too many assumptions about automatic enrollment.

If you receive Social Security when you turn 65 years old, you are automatically enrolled in Medicare Part A and/or Medicare Part B. If you are getting certain kinds of disability benefits from Social Security or the US Railroad Retirement Board (RRB), you are also automatically enrolled in Medicare Parts A and B after two years of disability benefits. If you have end-stage renal disease, you can apply for Medicare at any time as long as it coincides with being eligible for retirement benefits.

If you decided you don't want Medicare Part B, either because you have other insurance or you are covered through your own or your spouse's employer health plan, it is important to speak with someone to understand how your coverage works with Medicare and if there are any consequences to dropping Medicare Part B.

Enrollment in Medicare can be difficult, and there are specific times for specific events. It might be best to consult with a professional or the Medicare administration. Here is a brief explanation of the timing involved.

Medicare Initial Enrollment Period

Enrolling in Medicare Part A is automatic for most people. However, there are times where you may have to manually enroll in Medicare Part A and/ or Part B during your initial enrollment period (IEP). The IEP is a seven-month period that begins three months before you turn 65 years old, includes the month of your 65th birthday, and ends three months later.

Some situations where you would enroll in Medicare during your initial enrollment include the following:

- **If you aren't receiving retirement benefits:** If you are not yet receiving Social Security but you are close to your 65th birthday, you can sign up for Medicare Part A and/or Part B during your IEP. If you choose to delay your Social Security or RRB retirement benefits beyond age 65, you can apply for Medicare and then apply for retirement benefits sometime in the future.

- **If you do not qualify for retirement benefits:** If you are not eligible for retirement benefits from Social Security or the RRB, you will not be automatically enrolled into Original Medicare. However, you can still sign up for Medicare Part A and/or Part B during your IEP. Your Medicare Part A might come with a cost, which will depend on how long you paid Medicare taxes and worked.

Medicare General Enrollment Period

If you did not enroll during the IEP when you first became eligible for Medicare, you can enroll during something called the general enrollment period. The general enrollment period for Medicare runs from January 1 through March 31 of each year. Sometimes there is a late-enrollment penalty if you failed to sign up when you were first eligible.

Medicare Special Enrollment Period

There are times when you decide that your group medical insurance through an employer is good enough and you choose not to enroll in Medicare Part B. If you later lose your insurance or if you decide you want to switch to Medicare, you can sign up at any time when you are still covered by the group plan or during a special enrollment period. The special enrollment period is an eight-month period that begins either the month your employment ends or when your group health coverage ends, whichever happens first. Usually there are no late-enrollment penalty fees.

Medicare Advantage Enrollment

Medicare Advantage, or Medicare Part C, is provided through approved private insurance companies. All Medicare Advantage plans offer the same Medicare Part A and/or Part B benefits as Medicare. You must have Original Medicare Parts A and B to enroll in Medicare Advantage through a private insurer. There are two enrollment periods for Medicare Advantage: the initial coverage election period (ICEP) and annual election period.

MEDICARE ADVANTAGE INITIAL ENROLLMENT PERIOD

ICEP starts three months before you have Medicare Part A and Medicare Part B. The ICEP ends on whichever of the following dates is later:

- The last day of the month before you have Medicare Part A and Part B
- The last day of your Medicare Part B IEP

If you're under 65 and eligible for Medicare due to a disability, your ICEP will vary depending on when your disability benefits started.

MEDICARE ADVANTAGE ANNUAL ELECTION PERIOD

You can also add, drop, or change your Medicare Advantage plan during the annual election period, which occurs from October 15 through December 7 of every year. During this period, you may do the following:

- Switch from Original Medicare to Medicare Advantage and vice versa
- Switch from one Medicare Advantage plan to a different one
- Switch from a Medicare Advantage plan without prescription drug coverage to a Medicare Advantage plan that covers prescription drugs and vice versa

There are also supplement insurance policies that bridge gaps between Original Medicare and other expenses, such as deductibles, copayments, and coinsurance. These so-called "medigap" policies generally allow you to go to doctors or hospitals that accept Medicare. Medicare then pays its share of your costs and the medigap policies will pay their share.

Every situation is different, and your employer or spouse's employer coverage may be sufficient for a time. If you and your spouse are both not working, learn about and research your options. Read about the different enrollment periods and see the types of supplemental coverage you may think you need. Remember, Medicare is not free and should be considered as you budget your expenses into retirement.

The final step in this book will discuss health and health complication issues that could affect your retirement.

MEDICARE ENROLLMENT PERIOD CHECKLIST

8 MONTHS PRIOR TO 65

☐ Start learning about Medicare and Social Security.

☐ Determine your eligibility for Social Security and Medicare.

☐ Consider coverage options not included in Medicare.

☐ Find out if your doctors accept Medicare. Talk to family and friends about their experience with Medicare.

5 MONTHS PRIOR TO 65

☐ Speak with your employer to see whether group health coverage is an option.

☐ Identify the type of extra Medicare coverage that is right for you.

☐ Narrow your choice of insurers. If you've already made your decision on a Medicare supplement insurance plan, you can enroll now.

3 MONTHS PRIOR TO 65

☐ Apply for your Medicare benefits through the Social Security Administration. (This is the first month you are eligible to apply.)

☐ Determine if and how you are covered if you plan to travel within the United States or abroad.

☐ Learn how these plans would affect your selection of doctors.

☐ Ask about the plans' Medicare Part D coverage, including:

 ▪ Monthly premiums

 ▪ Copays/coinsurance

 ▪ Coverage for the drugs you currently take

 ▪ Possible conveniences such as mail-order pharmacy services

☐ Ask whether the plans offer hearing and vision discounts or dental coverage options.

☐ Sign up for Social Security if you've decided to take early Social Security benefits. (It usually takes three months after you sign up before you begin receiving benefits.)

SOURCE: Adapted from www.medicare.gov.

MEDICARE ENROLLMENT PERIOD CHECKLIST (CONTINUED)

2 MONTHS (OR 1 MONTH) PRIOR TO 65

☐ Decide whether you want Medicare Part B medical insurance. If not, have you returned the form that Medicare sent you indicating that you decline Part B coverage? (Most people take Part B.)

☐ Check to see if your doctor participates in Medicare and in Medicare Advantage plans, if appropriate.

☐ Select and sign up for an insurance policy that supplements Medicare or otherwise covers you if you think you need more protection.

☐ Check with your benefit coordinator at your job to be sure that both your retirement and health insurance transitions will go smoothly.

65 MONTH OF YOUR 65TH BIRTHDAY

During the month of your 65 birthday, make sure you've done the following:

☐ **Discuss your situation with your employer.** If you are still covered by your employer's health care plan after your 65th birthday, you should compare your premiums and other costs with that plan vs. the costs of paying for Medicare Part B and a Medicare Supplement or Medicare Advantage insurance policy. Surprisingly, the latter may be more economical.

Even if you continue to be covered by your employer, you should apply for Medicare Part A to supplement your employer's plan. You will receive a guide, *Medicare & You*, from the Centers for Medicare & Medicaid Services that explains your options and how they work.

In addition, call **800-MEDICARE** or **TTY: 1-877-486-2048** to request *Enrolling in Medicare*, or go to **www.medicare.gov**, "Search Tools," and then "Find a Medicare Publication." This guide explains your rights if you wish to enroll in Medicare Part B later.

☐ **Received your Medicare card.** Make sure you check it to verify your name and the coverage you want. Sign the card, make a copy for your files, and keep it in a safe place.

☐ **Sign the form that Medicare sent along with the card and return it if you don't want Part B.** You'll get another card indicating that you have only part A coverage. Sign it, make a copy for your files, and keep it in a safe place.

☐ **Ask your physicians whether they participate in Medicare or your preferred Medicare Advantage plan option.** This means they accept Medicare assignment or Medicare's allowable rates as payment in full.

☐ **Tell your physician to send your bills to Medicare if you sign up for Original Medicare or to any new Medicare plan you may have.**

☐ **Make arrangements for your spouse.** This is particularly important if her or she was covered by your employer's health plan. Such coverage is still a possibility.

☐ **Consider signing up for a Medicare Supplement or Medicare Advantage Insurance policy.** This is key. These policies can reduce your out-of-pocket expenses by picking up where Original medicare coverage leaves off.

SOURCE: Adapted from www.medicare.gov.

STEP

RESPECT YOUR HEALTH

One of the most important things you can do as you go through the retirement journey is to be honest with yourself. Be honest about your saving habits, your spending habits, and your ability to change any of those habits if you need to along the way.

At the very top of the honesty list should be your health. Be honest about how you take care of yourself and your ability to care for yourself later in life. If you don't make your health a priority, your retirement may become a much more complicated and difficult period for you and those around you.

Of course, health concerns may arise that are out of your control. Even if this is the case, you can also maintain a healthy lifestyle to prolong your life and make it as comfortable as possible in your retirement years.

According to a Merrill Lynch report titled "Health and Retirement: Planning for the Great Unknown," healthcare challenges pose a double threat to your retirement. First, expenses can be high, unpredictable, and deplete your retirement savings quickly. Second, if you are forced to retire early because of health issues, you will lose earning years and savings potential.

ESTIMATE OF OUT-OF-POCKET HEALTH CARE COSTS

The chart below shows an estimate of out-of-pocket healthcare costs based on one's estimated length of retirment in years.

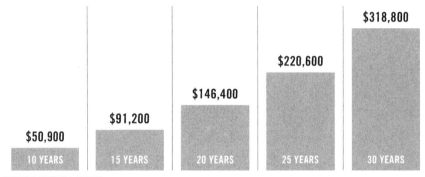

SOURCE: MERRILL LYNCH

The report points out an AARP (American Association of Retired Persons) survey that found two-thirds of large companies offered health benefits to retirees 25 years ago. Today, only one-third of large companies offer retirement health benefits.

As shown in the chart above, the longer you live past age 65, the greater the out-of-pocket expenses you will pay for healthcare. It's a difficult position to be in, even if you have done everything "right" in your savings and retirement budgeting.

The Role of Health Complications

Let's start with the good news. According to the Merrill Lynch Report, retirees say health is the number one factor in a happy retirement. Also, as the Baby Boomer generation ages and retires, many of them are taking a much more active involvement in their own health and the healthcare system on which they will depend.

Compared to their parents' generation, Baby Boomers are:

- More than four times more likely to say they actively research health information (79 percent versus 18 percent)

- Two-and-a-half times more likely to say they are proactive about their health (75 percent versus 30 percent)

- More than twice as likely to say they question doctors' orders (70 percent versus 29 percent)

- Twice as likely to say they view their doctor as an ally or partner who works with them to optimize their health (46 percent versus 23 percent)

Generational thinking is shifting to some degree, and Americans are changing the way they think about health as they age and begin to need healthcare.

The bad news begins when health complications occur. The US Department of Health and Human Services says that nearly 40 percent of people over the age of 65 years will spend time in a nursing home. Thirty percent will stay less than three months, but 50 percent stay more than a year and 20 percent stay longer than five years.

What does this mean for you and your retirement? It means that healthcare and long-term care is a reality you can't avoid, so it must be part of your savings strategy. AARP provides a calculator to determine if you are saving enough to provide for your healthcare in retirement (see Resources, page 133).

Long-Term Care

One thing to think about is how best to incorporate long-term care into your retirement-budgeting process. As you know, Medicare is not free, and it does not cover all your needs. Plus, average nursing home stays are more than two years, so you have to consider adding a budget of an extra $200,000 (not including inflation) into your savings. Working with your financial planner and/or accountant may help. Even if you don't need a nursing home, extra help and home healthcare costs add up, with some estimates at $40,000 per year. This is the self-insuring process where you save what you need. What else can you do?

If you decide to get long-term care insurance and pay premiums in exchange for healthcare services, you will need to consider a few things:

- **Amount of coverage:** You want to get as much coverage as possible, assuming the premiums are the same.

- **Premiums:** They can go up, and they often will. Make sure you are ready for this inevitability and how it affects your budgets and savings if it happens.

- **Benefits versus risks:** You may decide to take out long-term insurance and never use it. This will cost a lot of money that could have been spent elsewhere. You will want to weigh the risk of not needing insurance versus the benefits of it when you do need it. You may be happy that you purchased the insurance after you get the medical bills.

Some people will opt for long-term insurance that is used in conjunction with their life insurance policies. A so-called "hybrid" long-term care insurance will provide health coverage over and above your death benefit. Any money used for long-term care will reduce your death benefit first.

You also can purchase life insurance with a long-term care rider. This is similar to the hybrid policy, but the coverage is limited to the amount of your life insurance death benefit.

These are very personal decisions, and there is no right answer that fits everyone. You may be healthy today and may continue to be healthy throughout your retirement. You just don't know how things will turn out. As you talk with your financial planner about a proper saving strategy, consider these important areas of spending. See if you can afford it and how best to save for the long-term care of yourself and/or your spouse.

When planning for long-term healthcare, consider the timing of your decision. Insurance premiums are lower the younger you start (e.g., 55 rather than 70). Your health will be better when you are younger and not affect your ability to getting long-term health insurance policies. Also, if you are still working when you take out the policy, that income can help you pay for premiums into retirement.

Thinking about it sooner rather than later will help you better prepare for the worst while hoping for the best. The plan will have already been made and incorporated into your budget, and you will be acting rather than reacting when it is too late.

The Merrill Lynch study discusses the following steps to prepare for retirement healthcare expenses both for pre-retirees and retirees:

- Maintain a healthy lifestyle and wellness regimen. Even if you start later in life, the improvements you make can help you maintain good health in your retirement years.
- Take proactive steps to stay financially prepared for healthcare expenses.
- Estimate and begin saving for out-of-pocket healthcare expenses.
  - Learn as much as you can about Medicare and what it can and can't do for you.
  - Make sure you plan for lost income if you fall ill unexpectedly before retirement.
  - Talk to your family and advisor about healthcare topics and decisions.
  - Create contingency plans for healthcare problems and expenses for yourself and your spouse.
  - Research all long-term care options and prepare for your needs as best as you can.

Other Options

If you are under the age of 65, do not have Medicare, and are not covered through an employer, the Affordable Care Act allows enrollment through its Health Insurance Marketplace so you can buy insurance that fits your needs. Open enrollment has come and gone, but there are special enrollment periods. There is also potential for tax credits and lower out-of-pocket costs depending on your income and household size.

If you have coverage through an employer, you are considered covered under the law.

If you have retiree coverage and want to buy a Marketplace plan instead, you can. However, you will want to note the following:

- You won't get lower costs on Marketplace coverage.
- If you voluntarily discontinue your retiree coverage, you won't qualify for a special enrollment period to enroll in a new Marketplace plan.

> ## BY THE NUMBERS
>
> The Merrill Lynch study found that while financial planning should include discussions around healthcare and how best to prepare, it generally does not.
>
> - Less than 15 percent (one in six) pre-retirees have attempted to estimate how much money they might need for healthcare in retirement.
> - Seven percent of people aged 55–64 years say they feel knowledgeable about Medicare coverage.
> - Among Medicare recipients, 19 percent say they feel knowledgeable about Medicare offerings.

- You won't be able to enroll in health coverage through the Marketplace until the next open enrollment period.

If you are older than the age of 65, refer to Step 7 where Medicare, its eligibility requirements, and automatic enrollment for certain types of plans is described in detail. Other plans can be purchased for greater coverage.

Health Savings Accounts

Saving for healthcare can be a daunting task, especially given all the saving that's just associated with living expenses. If you have exhausted Medicare and your own savings options, there are other alternatives that can help you pay for medical expenses.

Health savings accounts (HSAs) are personal savings accounts that allow you to put money (sometimes pretax and sometimes posttax) into an account to pay for medical expenses. The best part is that the money contributed to the plan is not subject to federal income tax when you deposit it, as it grows, or when you withdraw it, providing you a "triple tax savings." Sometimes employers offer these plans to employees, and the money can be rolled over, when needed, to other HSAs.

An HSA can provide you with the following:

- Control of how much money to put away, which expenses to pay, where to hold the money, and how to invest it.

- The money belongs to you, and there are no "use it or lose it" rules.

- Your contributions are allowed as a tax deduction.
- Your contributions can be excluded from your gross income.
- You can use HSA money to pay for current or future medical expenses.

However, there are certain qualifications to be eligible to open an HSA. The IRS says you must be covered under a high-deductible health plan, have no other health coverage, not be enrolled in Medicare, and not be claimed as a dependent.

Also, once you turn 65, you can no longer contribute to your HSA. You can take money out of it tax-free. Much like 401(k)s, employer HSAs offer investment options that can involve risk and loss. It's best not to put all your HSA money into one type of investment. This is money for medical expenses, and you'll want it when you need it. Think of your stage in life, just as you would with your 401(k), and choose investments that reflect your risk tolerances and goals.

HSAs should not be confused with **flexible spending accounts (FSAs)**, which do not allow you to roll over money you have not used. They are accounts with finite periods of time to use them. You can use FSAs to pay healthcare bills, but you will lose the money if you don't use it before the year's end.

Asking the Right Questions

Despite everything you have read in this chapter, when it comes to healthcare considerations, everything depends on you. What kind of consumer are you? Are you asking the right questions? Are you asking them of the right people? Are you getting the information you need to be informed and educated?

These are the most important steps you must take, even with the provisions of Medicare, savings, and HSAs. It is important to identify the best, most cost-effective providers to manage your care into retirement. Fidelity Investments discusses four types of providers you should identify for the best care possible.

- A primary physician
- A specialist for any existing conditions

- An urgent care provider
- A full-service hospital

Fidelity also recommends that you are prepared to give your provider information. Ask the hard questions to get a clear description of any diagnosis and the doctor's proposed plan. And know what you are paying for—the fees, charges, and out-of-pocket costs you can expect for treatments or recommended treatments.

The bottom line is to prepare for any possibility. You may feel well today, but you don't know what is lurking down the road. Medical costs can be extremely high, so solid savings and preparation, just as with your retirement savings, will save you from added stress and debt later on. When considering your health needs, hoping for the best and preparing for the worst has never been truer.

Conclusion

The eight steps in this book are by no means exhaustive, but you are now on your way to retirement with the right roadmap. How you use this map and the turns and shortcuts you make are your own decisions. Make sure your choices fit your future lifestyles and needs. There is no one-size-fits-all solution, but this is a good start. You can look at the map and say, "I see how I can get to point B." As long as the journey is becoming clearer, other things will fall into place. Give yourself time and expect frustrations, down-markets, and bad choices. Remember, it is never too late, and you are never too old to start this journey. Take a deep breath and take another step. I wish you good luck.

Glossary

"4 percent" rule: The 4 percent rule seeks to provide a steady stream of funds to the retiree while also keeping an account balance that will allow funds to be withdrawn for a number of years. The 4 percent rate is considered to be a "safe" rate, with the withdrawals consisting primarily of interest and dividends.

annuity: An annuity is a contract between you and an insurance company that requires the insurer to make payments to you, either immediately or in the future. You buy an annuity by making either a single payment or a series of payments. Similarly, your payout may come either as one lump-sum payment or as a series of payments over time.

asset allocation: Asset allocation involves dividing an investment portfolio among different asset categories, such as stocks, bonds, and cash. The asset allocation that works best for you at any given point in your life will depend largely on your time horizon and your ability to tolerate risk.

average indexed monthly earnings: Your average indexed monthly earnings takes your top 35 highest-earning years up to age 60, indexes it for wage growth, and then averages it to get a monthly amount. It tries to approximate your earnings over your lifetime at today's wage levels.

bond: A bond is a debt security, similar to an IOU. When you buy a bond, you are lending to the issuer, which may be a government, municipality, or corporation. In return, the issuer promises to pay you a specified rate of interest during the life of the bond and repay the principal when it "matures," or comes due after a set period of time.

budget: An estimation of the revenue and expenses over a specified future period of time. A budget can be made for a person, family, group of people, business, government, country, multinational organization, or just about any other entity that makes and spends money.

common stock: A security that represents ownership in a corporation. Holders of common stock exercise control by electing a board of directors and voting on corporate policy.

compounding: Interest calculated on the initial principal and also on the accumulated interest of previous periods of a deposit or loan. Compound interest can be thought of as "interest on interest." It will make a deposit or loan grow at a faster rate than simple interest, which is interest calculated only on the principal amount.

Consumer Price Index (inflation): A measure that examines the changes in the price of a basket of goods and services purchased by urban consumers.

cost-of-living adjustment: An adjustment made to Social Security in order to adjust benefits to counteract the effects of inflation. Cost-of-living adjustments are generally equal to the percentage increase in the Consumer Price Index.

debt: An amount owed to a person or organization for borrowed funds. Loans, notes, bonds, and mortgages are forms of debt. These different forms all call for borrowers to pay back the amount they owe, typically with interest, by a specific date, which is set forth in the repayment terms.

defined benefit (DB) plan: DB plans also are known as pension plans. Employers sponsor DB plans and promise the plan's investments will provide you with a specified monthly benefit at retirement. The employer bears the investment risks.

defined contribution (DC) plan: A retirement savings plan, such as a 401(k) plan, that does not promise a specific payment upon retirement. In these plans, the employee or the employer (or both) contribute to the employee's individual account. The employee bears the investment risks.

discretionary spending: The money you spend on nonessentials such as luxury items and travel.

diversification: A risk-management technique that mixes a wide variety of investments within a portfolio. The rationale for diversification is that a portfolio of different kinds of investments will, on average, yield higher returns and pose a lower risk than any individual investment found within the portfolio.

dividends: A distribution of a portion of a company's earnings, decided on by the board of directors. The dividend is most often quoted in terms of the dollar amount each share receives (dividends per share).

equity REIT: A type of REIT that gets most of its revenue from rent.

essential spending: The amount you spend on essential items such as food, shelter, and clothing.

exchange-traded funds (ETF): Like mutual funds, ETFs offer investors a way to pool their money in a fund that makes investments in stocks, bonds, or other assets. Unlike mutual funds, ETF shares are traded on a national stock exchange.

financial planner: An investment professional who typically prepares financial plans for clients. The services financial planners offer can vary from assessing every aspect of a client's financial life to only being able to recommend investments.

flexible spending account (FSA): A type of savings account available that provides you with specific tax advantages. Set up by an employer for an employee, the account allows employees to contribute a portion of their regular earnings to pay for qualified expenses, such as medical expenses or dependent care expenses.

full retirement age (FRA): The age at which you are eligible for full retirement benefits from the government. The age used to be 65 but if you were born after 1942, your full retirement age is 66. If you were born after 1960, it's 67.

Government Pension Offset: Government Pension Offsets apply to government workers at any level who are not covered by Social Security. Any federal, state, or local employee who works for a governmental institution in any capacity and is eligible to receive a separate retirement pension from his or her employer is subject to this offset. The offset will reduce by two-thirds the amount of spousal and/or survivor benefits that the surviving spouse or beneficiary would have been entitled to if he or she were eligible for Social Security.

Great Recession: The term "Great Recession" applies to both the US recession, officially lasting from December 2007 to June 2009, and the ensuing global recession in 2009. The economic slump began when the US housing market collapsed.

health savings account (HSA): An account created for individuals who are covered under high-deductible health plans to save for medical expenses that the plans do not cover. Contributions are made into the account by you or your employer and are limited to a maximum amount each year. The contributions are invested over time and can be used to pay for qualified medical expenses.

individual retirement account (IRA): An investing tool used by individuals to earn and earmark funds for retirement savings.

Medicaid: A joint federal and state program that helps low-income individuals or families pay for the costs associated with long-term medical and custodial care.

Medicare: A federal health insurance program, administered by the Social Security Administration, that provides healthcare for older adults.

mortgage REIT: A type of REIT that gets most of its revenue from interest on mortgages or mortgage-backed securities.

mutual fund: An investment that is made up of a pool of funds collected from many investors for the purpose of investing in securities, such as stocks, bonds, money market instruments, and similar assets.

preferred stock: A class of ownership in a corporation that has a higher claim on the assets and earnings than common stock. Preferred stock generally has a dividend that must be paid out before dividends to common stockholders, but ownership of the shares usually do not allow for the investor to have voting rights in regard to the corporation's dealings and board.

primary insurance amount: A calculation, used in conjunction with average indexed monthly earnings, to determine a person's Social Security benefits.

private equity: Private equity consists of investors and funds that make investments directly into private companies or conduct buyouts of public companies that result in a delisting of a public equity.

real estate investment trusts (REITs): A security that sells like a stock on the major exchanges and invests in real estate directly, either through properties or mortgages.

required minimum distribution (RMD): A required minimum distribution is the amount the federal government requires you to withdraw each year, usually after you reach age 70 ½, from retirement accounts, including IRAs, as well as many employer-sponsored retirement plans.

risk: The chance that an investment's actual return will be different than expected. Risk includes the possibility of losing some or all of your original investment.

Roth IRA: An individual retirement account that bears many similarities to the traditional IRA, but contributions are not tax deductible and qualified distributions are tax-free.

sandwich generation: A generation of people, typically in their 30s or 40s, responsible for bringing up their own children and the care of their aging parents.

Social Security: A US federal program of social insurance and benefits developed in 1935. The Social Security program benefits include retirement income, disability income, Medicare, and Medicaid, and death and survivorship benefits.

subprime mortgage: A type of mortgage that is normally made out to borrowers with lower credit ratings. As a result of the borrower's lowered credit rating, a conventional mortgage is not offered because the lender views the borrower as having a larger-than-average risk of defaulting on the loan.

target-date/life-cycle funds: A target-date fund is an investment fund that allows you to link your investment portfolio to a particular time horizon, which is typically your expected retirement date.

tax-deferred: Investments on which applicable taxes (typically income taxes and capital gains taxes) are paid at a future date instead of in the period in which they are incurred.

"three-bucket" strategy: The principle of the bucket strategy is to allocate the portfolio toward three defined buckets: The risk-free bucket, the risk-off bucket, and the risk-on bucket. The role of each bucket is to allocate the capital toward these three defined roles.

"three-legged stool:" A description of the three most common sources of retirement income for a retiree: Social Security, personal savings, and employer savings plans.

US Securities and Exchange Commission: A government commission created by Congress to regulate the securities markets and protect investors.

volatility: Unpredictable and vigorous changes in prices within the stock market.

Resources

STOCKS, MUTUAL FUNDS, AND FINANCIAL MARKET ANALYSIS

- Bloomberg.com
- Finance.yahoo.com
- Google.com/finance
- Money.cnn.com
- Money.msn.com
- Morningstar.com
- Nasdaq.com
- NYSE.com
- Stockcharts.com

BONDS

- Investinginbonds.com
- Markets.ft.com
- Morningstar.com

FINANCIAL PLANNING RESOURCES

- Certified Financial Planner Board of Standards (CFP.net)
- The National Association of Personal Financial Advisors (NAPFA.org)
- US Securities and Exchange Commission (Fast Answers: Financial Planners—SEC.gov/answers/finplan.htm)

BUDGETING AND FINANCING APPS

- BDGT.com
- BillGuard.com
- Mint.com
- Mvelopes.com
- Spendeeapp.com
- YouNeedABudget.com

OTHER RESOURCES

- Internal Revenue Service (for tax issues—IRS.gov)
- The Official US Government Site for Medicare (Medicare.gov)
- Social Security (SSA.gov)

CALCULATORS

- AARP (Healthcare Costs Calculator: AARP.org/work/retirement -planning/the-aarp-healthcare-costs-calculator)
- Financial Industry Regulatory Authority (FINRA) (Required Minimum Distribution Calculator: apps.finra.org/Calcs/1/RMD)
- Social Security (Benefit Calculators: SocialSecurity.gov/OACT/quickcalc /index.html)
- US Department of Agriculture (Cost of Raising a Child Calculator: CNPP.usda.gov/tools/CRC_Calculator/default.aspx)
- US Securities and Exchange Commission (Compound Interest Calculator: Investor.gov/tools/calculators/compound-interest-calculator# .VAfKiEuA_Wg)
- Vanguard (Retirement Expenses Calculator: personal.vanguard.com /us/insights/retirement/tool/retirement-expense-worksheet)

FURTHER READING

Barry, Patricia. *Medicare for Dummies.* Hoboken, NJ: John Wiley & Sons, 2014.

Collie, Bob, Don Ezra, and Matthew X. Smith. *The Retirement Plan Solution: The Reinvention of Defined Contribution.* Hoboken, NJ: John Wiley & Sons, 2009.

Eisenberg, Lee. *The Number: A Completely Different Way to Think About the Rest of Your Life.* New York, NY: Simon & Schuster, 2006.

Jason, Julie. *The AARP Retirement Guide: How to Make Smart Financial Decisions in Good Times and Bad.* New York, NY: Sterling Publishing, 2009.

Maurer, Tim, and Jim Stovall. *The Ultimate Financial Plan: Balancing Your Money and Life.* Hoboken, NJ: John Wiley & Sons, 2011.

Mindel, Norbert M. and Sharon E. Sleight. *Wealth Management in the New Economy: Investor Strategies for Growing, Protecting, and Transferring Wealth.* Hoboken, NJ: John Wiley & Sons, 2010

Piper, Mike. *Social Security Made Simple: Social Security Retirement Benefits and Related Planning Topics Explained in 100 Pages or Less.* St. Louis, MO: Simple Subjects, 2012.

References

STEP ONE

Arends, Brett. "Retirement 101: How to Figure Out What You'll Need." *The Wall Street Journal*. Updated March 23, 2011. Accessed August 9, 2015. http://online .wsj.com/news/articles/SB10001424052748703410604576216950781576840.

Bankrate. "February 2013 Financial Security Index Charts." Accessed August 9, 2015. www.bankrate.com/finance/consumer-index/financial-security-charts-0213.aspx.

BlackRock. "Retirement Expense Worksheet." Accessed August 9, 2105. www.blackrock.com/investing/literature/investor-education/retirement -expense-worksheet-education-va-us.pdf.

Employee Benefit Research Institute. "The 2013 EBRI-Greenwald Retirement Confidence Survey: Part I." June 10, 2013. Accessed August 9, 2015. www.retirement-insight.com/the-2013-ebri-greenwald-retirement-confidence -survey-part-i/.

Federal Research Division, Library of Congress. "Financial Literacy Among Retail Investors in the United States." December 30, 2011. Accessed August 10, 2015. www.sec.gov/news/studies/2012/917-financial-literacy-study-part2.pdf.

Fidelity. "Retiree Health Costs Hold Steady." June 11, 2014. Accessed August 9, 2015. www.fidelity.com/viewpoints/retirement/retirees-medical-expenses.

Kadlec, Dan. "Redefining the 'Ideal' Retirement." *Time*. August 29, 2013. Accessed August 9, 2015. http://business.time.com/2013/08/29/redefining-the-ideal -retirement/.

Kaiser Family Foundation, Health Research & Educational Trust. "Employer Health Benefits: 2013 Annual Survey." August 2013. Accessed August 9, 2015. http:// kaiserfamilyfoundation.files.wordpress.com/2013/08/8465-employer-health -benefits-20132.pdf.

Nationwide. "Understanding Inflation." Accessed August 10, 2015. www.nrsforu.com /iApp/tcm/nrsforu/learning/library/inflation.jsp.

Skowronski, Jeannine. "America's Best Savers Are Not the Wealthy." Bankrate. March 30, 2015. Accessed August 10, 2015. www.bankrate.com/finance /consumer-index/americas-best-savers-are-not-the-wealthy.aspx?ic_id=Top _Financial%20News%20Center_link_4.

Social Security Administration. "Retirement Planner: Benefits by Year of Birth." Accessed August 9, 2015. www.socialsecurity.gov/retire2/agereduction.htm.

Social Security Administration. "Social Security Basic Facts." April 2, 2014. Accessed August 9, 2015. www.ssa.gov/news/press/basicfact.html.

US Department of Agriculture. "Expenditures on Children by Families." Accessed September 19, 2015. http://www.cnpp.usda.gov /ExpendituresonChildrenbyFamilies

US Department of Labor. "Consumer Price Index." Accessed August 9, 2015. www.bls.gov/cpi/.

STEP TWO

AARP. "Social Security Alone Isn't Enough." www.aarp.org/work/social-security /info-06-2010/ss_isnt_enough.html.

Bdgt. "Bdgt.me: Smarter Budgets." Accessed August 9, 2015. www.bdgt.me.

Bernard, Tara Siegel. "Make a Resolution Budget: Here Are Some Apps to Help." *The New York Times.* January 3, 2014. Accessed August 9, 2015. www.nytimes.com /2014/01/04/your-money/household-budgeting/review-apps-to-track-income -and-expenses.html?_r=0&gwh=DD3A0B3F5DC8FC1D335E293F09E6E7E2 &gwt=pay.

Deloitte. "Meeting the Retirement Challenge: New Approaches and Solutions for the Financial Services Industry." Accessed August 9, 2015. www2.deloitte.com /content/dam/Deloitte/us/Documents/financial-services/us-fsi-meeting-the -retirement-challenge-09302014.pdf.

Desilver, Drew. "Five Facts About Social Security." Pew Research Center. October 16, 2013. Accessed August 9, 2015. www.pewresearch.org/fact-tank/2013/10/16 /5-facts-about-social-security/.

Dunham, Troy. "Poll: How Husbands and Wives Really Feel About Their Finances." *Money.* June 1, 2014. Accessed August 9, 2015. http://time.com/money/2800576 /love-money-by-the-numbers/.

Employee Benefit Research Institute. "The 2013 EBRI-Greenwald Retirement
   Confidence Survey: Part I." June 10, 2013. Accessed August 9, 2015.
   www.retirement-insight.com/the-2013-ebri-greenwald-retirement-confidence
   -survey-part-i/.

Financial Mentor. "Twenty-Seven Retirement Savings Catch Up Strategies for Late
   Starters (Part 1)." Accessed August 9, 2015. http://financialmentor.com
   /free-articles/retirement-planning/saving-for-retirement/27-retirement
   -savings-catch-up-strategies-for-late-starters-part-1.

Investopedia. "Compounding." Accessed August 9, 2015. www.investopedia.com
   /terms/c/compounding.asp.

Luxenberg, Stan. "A Retirement Strategy for Nervous Investors." Nasdaq. Accessed
   August 9, 2015. www.nasdaq.com/personal-finance/retirement-strategy
   -nervous-investors.aspx.

Morningstar. "Historical Volatility." Accessed August 9, 2015. www.morningstar.com
   /InvGlossary/historical_volatility.aspx

National Poverty Center. "The Effects of the Great Recession on the Retirement
   Security of Older Workers." March 2013. Accessed August 9, 2015. http://
   npc.umich.edu/publications/u/2013-03-npc-working-paper.pdf.

Prudential. "Retirement Challenges." Accessed August 9, 2015. http://incomecertainty
   .prudential.com/retirement-challenges.aspx.

Russell Investments. "The Magic of Compounding." Accessed August 9, 2015.
   www.russell.com/us/individual-investors/why-invest/getting-started
   /compounding.page.

Standard Bank. "Financial Goals for Each Stage of Your Life." March 26, 2014.
   Accessed August 9, 2015. www.blog.standardbank.com/node/54798.

US Securities and Exchange Commission. "Compound Interest Calculator."
   Accessed August 9, 2015. www.investor.gov/tools/calculators/compound
   -interest-calculator#.VAfKiEuA_Wg.

Wells Fargo. "Middle Class Americans Face a Retirement Shutdown; 37% Say
   'I'll Never Retire, but Work Until I'm Too Sick or Die,' a Wells Fargo Study Finds."
   October 23, 2013. Accessed August 9, 2015. www.wellsfargo.com/about/press
   /2013/20131023_middleclasssurvey.

Wells Fargo. "Retirement Planning." Accessed August 9, 2015. www.wellsfargo.com
   /retirementplan/planning/.

STEP THREE

BusinessDictionary.com. "Private Equity: Definition." Accessed August 9, 2015. www.businessdictionary.com/definition/private-equity.html.

Charles Schwab. "Investing Basics: 2. Plan Your Mix." Accessed August 9, 2015. www.schwab.com/public/schwab/investing/retirement_and_planning/how_to _invest/investing_basics/plan_your_mix.

CIBC. "What Is a Mutual Fund." Accessed August 9, 2015. www.cibc.com/ca/advice -centre/new-to-canada/what-is-a-mutual-fund.html.

CNN Money. "Stocks: Investing in Stocks." May 28, 2015. Accessed August 9, 2015. http://money.cnn.com/magazines/moneymag/money101/lesson5/index2.htm.

Consumer Federation of America. "2012 Household Financial Planning Survey." July 23, 2012. Accessed August 9, 2015. www.consumerfed.org/pdfs/Studies.CFA -CFPBoardReport7.23.12.pdf.

Daily Courier. "US Construction Spending Rebounds 1.8 Percent in July, Biggest Gain in More Than 2 Years." September 2, 2014. Accessed August 9, 2015. www.kelownadailycourier.ca/business_news/national_business/article _59c9af8d-8eb1-5da4-b8d8-a05321d70838.html.

Employee Benefit Research Institute. "Facts From EBRI: History of 401(k) Plans— an Update." Last modified February 2005. Accessed August 9, 2015. www.ebri.org /pdf/publications/facts/0205fact.a.pdf.

Employee Benefit Research Institute. "History of Pension Plans." March 1998. Accessed August 9, 2015. www.ebri.org/publications/facts/index.cfm?fa =0398afact.

Fidelity. "What Is an IRA?" Accessed August 9, 2015. www.fidelity.com/retirement -planning/learn-about-iras/what-is-an-ira.

Financial Planning Standards Council. "10 Questions to Ask Your Planner." Accessed August 9, 2015. www.fpsc.ca/10-questions-ask-your-planner#experience.

Forbes. "10 Questions to Ask a Financial Advisor." Accessed August 9, 2015. www.forbes.com/pictures/fjfi45edmi/8-how-much-contact-do-you-have-with -your-clients-2/.

Hughes, Emma Ann. "Pros and Cons of Exchange-Traded Funds." FT Adviser. September 26, 2013. Accessed August 9, 2015. www.ftadviser.com/2013/09/26 /investments/etfs-and-trackers/pros-and-cons-of-exchange-traded-funds -EpZPoscYaOhSz13fcBwMxI/article.html.

Investment Company Institute. "2014 Investment Company Fact Book." May 14, 2015. Accessed August 9, 2015. www.ici.org/pdf/2014_factbook.pdf.

Investopedia. "Definition of 'Stock.'" Accessed August 9, 2015. www.investopedia.com /terms/s/stock.asp.

Jacobe, Dennis. "Gold Loses Luster in U.S. as Investment; Real Estate Gains." Gallup. April 16, 2013. Accessed August 9, 2015. www.gallup.com/poll/161909/gold-loses -luster-investment-real-estate-gains.aspx.

Jacobe, Dennis. "In US, 54% Have Stock Market Investments, Lowest Since 1999." Gallup. April 20, 2011. Accessed August 9, 2015. www.gallup.com/poll/147206 /Stock-Market-Investments-Lowest-1999.aspx.

Malone, Matthew. "What Is a Roth IRA?" RothIRA.com. Accessed August 9, 2015. www.rothira.com/what-is-a-Roth-IRA.

Nasdaq.com. "What Are ETFs?" Accessed August 9, 2015. www.nasdaq.com/investing /etfs/what-are-etfs.aspx.

NBCNews.com. "11 Historic Bear Markets: From the Great Depression to the Great Recession." Accessed August 9, 2015. www.nbcnews.com/id/37740147/ns /business-stocks_and_economy/t/historic-bear-markets/#.VCtnNr427Wh.

Pension Benefit Guaranty Corporation. "History of PBGC." Accessed August 9, 2015. www.pbgc.gov/about/who-we-are/pg/history-of-pbgc.html.

Reit.com. "What Is a REIT?" Accessed August 9, 2015. www.reit.com/investing /reit-basics/what-reit.

Vogel, John. "Thinking Outside the Housing Bubble." *US News & World Report.* June 14, 2013. Accessed August 9, 2015. www.usnews.com/opinion/blogs/economic -intelligence/2013/06/14/housing-bubble-or-credit-bubble-it-matters.

Wall Street Journal. "How to Choose a Financial Planner." Accessed August 9, 2015. http://guides.wsj.com/personal-finance/managing-your-money/how-to -choose-a-financial-planner/.

Wall Street Journal. "What Is a Bond?" Accessed August 9, 2015. http:// guides.wsj.com/personal-finance/investing/what-is-a-bond/.

US Department of Labor. "Retirement Plans, Benefits & Savings: Types of Retire-ment Plans." Accessed August 9, 2015. www.dol.gov/dol/topic/retirement /typesofplans.htm.

STEP FOUR

Aon Hewitt. "Leakage of Participants' DC Assets: How Loans, Withdrawals, and Cahouts are Eroding Retirement Income 2011." Accessed August 9, 2015. www.aon.com/attachments/thought-leadership/survey_asset_leakage.pdf.

Aquire, Sally. "3 Reasons Why you Shouldn't Borrow From Your 401(k)." Money Crashers. Accessed August 9, 2015. www.moneycrashers.com/3-reasons-why-you -shouldnt-borrow-from-your-401k/.

AXA. "Borrowing or Withdrawing Money From Your 401(k) Plan." Accessed August 9, 2015. https://us.axa.com/retirement/borrowing-or-withdrawing-money -from-your-401k.html.

Charles Schwab. "What's the Best Way to Withdraw Money From My Savings?" Accessed August 9, 2015. www.schwab.com/public/schwab/investing /retirement_and_planning/retirement/retirement_advice/withdrawing _retirement_money/what_is_the_best_way_to_withdraw_money_from_my _savings.html.

Financial Industry Regulatory Authority. "Calculator." Accessed August 9, 2015. http://apps.finra.org/Calcs/1/RMD.

Financial Industry Regulatory Authority. "401(k) Loans, Hardship Withdrawals, and Other Important Considerations." Accessed August 10, 2015. www.finra.org /Investors/smartinvesting/retirement/smart401kinvesting/income/p125503.

Geary, Leslie. "Savvy Ways to Withdraw Retirement Funds." Fox Business. January 3, 2014. Accessed August 9, 2015. www.foxbusiness.com/personal-finance /2014/01/02/savvy-ways-to-withdraw-retirement-funds/.

Guillot, Craig. "Emergency Fund 101: How to Start Saving for a Rainy Day." Mint Life. January 10, 2013. Accessed August 9, 2015. www.mint.com/blog/saving /emergency-fund-101-how-to-start-saving-for-a-rainy-day-0113/.

IRS. "Do's and Don'ts of Hardship Distributions." Last modified June 19, 2015. Accessed August 9, 2015. www.irs.gov/Retirement-Plans/Do's-and-Don'ts-of -Hardship-Distributions.

IRS. "Retirement Plans FAQs Regarding Hardship Distributions." Last modified March 2, 2015. Accessed August 9, 2015. www.irs.gov/Retirement-Plans /Retirement-Plans-FAQs-regarding-Hardship-Distributions.

J.P. Morgan. "Executive Summary: Breaking the 4% Rule." Accessed August 9, 2015. www.jpmorganfunds.com/blobcontent/4/185/1323375351903_ES-DYNAMIC.pdf.

National Foundation for Credit Counseling. "Majority of Americans Do Not Have Money Available to Meet an Unplanned Expense." Accessed August 9, 2015. www.nfcc.org/majority-of-americans-do-not-have-money-available-to-meet -an-unplanned-expense/.

Ning, David. "7 Reasons Not to Use the 4% Rule." *US News & World Report.* December 19, 2015. Accessed August 9, 2015. http://money.usnews.com/money/blogs /on-retirement/2012/12/19/7-reasons-not-to-use-the-4-percent-rule.

Rosenthal, Larry. "How Much to Withdraw From Retirement Savings." *Forbes.* June 10, 2013. Accessed August 9, 2015. www.forbes.com/sites/nextavenue/2013/06 /10/how-much-to-withdraw-from-retirement-savings/.

Smith, Lisa. "8 Reasons to Never Borrow From Your 401(k)." Investopedia. Accessed August 9, 2015. www.investopedia.com/articles/retirement/06 /eightreasons401k.asp.

TIAA-CREF Financial Services. "Withdrawals From Retirement Plan." Accessed August 9, 2015. www1.tiaa-cref.org/public/support/help/ask-tiaa-cref /withdrawals-retirement-plan/index.html.

VenDerhei, Jack, Sarah Holden, Luis Alonso, and Steven Bass. "Issue Brief: 401(k) Plan Asset Allocation, Account Balances, and Loan Activity in 2011." Employee Benefit Research Institute. December 2012. Accessed August 9, 2015. www.ebri.org/pdf/briefspdf/EBRI_IB_12-2012_No380.401k-eoy2011.pdf.

Zimmerman, Eilene. "4% Rule for Retirement Withdrawals Is Golden no More." *The New York Times.* May 14, 2013. Accessed August 15, 2015. www.nytimes. com/2013/05/15/business/retirementspecial/the-4-rule-for-retirement -withdrawals-may-be-outdated.html.

STEP FIVE

BlackRock. "Understanding Social Security Retirement Benefits." Accessed August 9, 2015. www.blackrock.com/investing/literature/brochure/social-security -brochure-va-us.pdf.

Kiplinger. "Plan to Pay Taxes on Social Security." December 2012. Accessed August 9, 2015. www.kiplinger.com/article/retirement/T037-C000-S001-plan-to-pay -taxes-on-social-security.html.

National Academy of Social Insurance. "Short Answers to Common Questions About Social Security." May 2013. Accessed August 9, 2015. www.nasi.org/research /2013/short-answers-common-questions-about-social-security.

National Academy of Social Insurance. "What Is Social Security." Accessed August 9, 2015. www.nasi.org/learn/socialsecurity/overview.

Social Security Administration. "Benefits Planner: Social Security Credits." Accessed August 9, 2015. www.ssa.gov/retire2/credits.htm.

Social Security Administration. "Frequently Asked Questions." Accessed August 9, 2015. www.ssa.gov/history/hfaq.html.

Social Security Administration. "Retirement Planner: Getting Benefits While Working." Accessed August 9, 2105. www.ssa.gov/retire2/whileworking.htm.

Social Security Administration. "Retirement Planner: Maximum Taxable Earnings." Accessed August 9, 2015. www.ssa.gov/retire2/topwages.htm.

Social Security Online. "Social Security Quick Calculator." Accessed August 9, 2015. www.socialsecurity.gov/OACT/quickcalc/index.html.

Social Security Administration. "Survivors Benefits." July 2015. Accessed August 9, 2015. www.socialsecurity.gov/pubs/EN-05-10084.pdf.

Social Security Administration. "What Is the Best to Age to Start Your Benefits?" Accessed August 9, 2015. www.ssa.gov/retire2/otherthings.htm.

Social Security Administration. "When to Start Receiving Benefits." August 2015. Accessed August 9, 2015. www.ssa.gov/pubs/EN-05-10147.pdf.

Social Security Administration. "Your Noncovered Pension May Affect Your Benefits as Spouse or Widow/Widower." Accessed August 9, 2015. www.ssa.gov/retire2/gpo.htm.

STEP SIX

AARP. "Ready for Retirement? Tools to Achieve Peace of Mind: Social Security and Taxes." Accessed August 9, 2015. www.aarp.org/content/dam/aarp/work/social_security/2011-10/Social-Security-and-Taxes.pdf.

Ambrose, Eileen. "Avoid a Nasty Tax Surprise." AARP. September 2014. Accessed August 9, 2015. www.aarp.org/work/retirement-planning/info-2014/tax-deferred-retirement-savings-balance.3.html.

Ameriprise Financial. "Taxation of Investments." Accessed August 9, 2015. www.ameriprise.com/budgeting-investing/tax-center/tax-planning-tax-strategies/how-an-investment-is-taxed.asp.

CNN Money. "Ultimate Guide to Retirement." Accessed August 9, 2015. money.cnn.com/retirement/guide/?iid=EL.

Cussen, Mark P. "Will You Pay Taxes During Retirement?" Investopedia. November 22, 2011. Accessed August 9, 2015. www.investopedia.com/articles/retirement/12 /will-you-pay-taxes-during-retirement.asp.

Insured Retirement Institute. "Taxation of Annuities." Accessed August 9, 2015. www.irionline.org/government-affairs/annuities-regulation-industry -information/taxation-of-annuities.

IRS. "Are Your Social Security Benefits Taxable?" February 7, 2011. Accessed August 9, 2015. www.irs.gov/uac/Are-Your-Social-Security-Benefits-Taxable%3F.

IRS. "IRS Required Minimum Distribution Worksheet." Accessed August 9, 2015. www.irs.gov/pub/irs-tege/uniform_rmd_wksht.pdf.

Lee, Jeanne. "Taxes and Your Retirement Income." Wells Fargo. Accessed August 9, 2015. www.wellsfargo.com/beyondtoday/ages-stages/60s/retirementtaxes.

STEP SEVEN

Blue Cross Blue Shield of Massachusetts. "Medigap." Accessed August 10, 2015. https://www.bluecrossma.com/medicare-options/2015/medicare-plans/#msps.

eHealthMedicare. "Medicare Enrollment: How and When to Enroll in Medicare." Accessed August 9, 2015. www.ehealthmedicare.com/about-medicare/enrollment /b/?allid=Med35749.

Fidelity. "Retiree Health Costs Hold Steady." June 11, 2014. Accessed August 9, 2015. www.fidelity.com/viewpoints/retirement/retirees-medical-expenses.

Medicare.gov. "How Is Medicare Funded?" Accessed August 9, 2015. www.medicare .gov/about-us/how-medicare-is-funded/medicare-funding.html.

Medicare.gov. "Medicare 2014 Costs at a Glance." Accessed August 9, 2015. www.medicare.gov/your-medicare-costs/costs-at-a-glance/costs-at-glance.html.

Medicare.gov. "Medicare and You: 2015." Last modified December 2014. Accessed August 9, 2015. www.medicare.gov/Pubs/pdf/10050.pdf.

Tavenner, Marilyn. "Medicare and Medicaid Forty-Nine Years and Stronger." HHS.gov/HealthCare. July 30, 2014. Accessed August 9, 2015. www.hhs.gov /healthcare/facts/blog/2014/07/medicare-and-medicaid-forty-nine-years -and-stronger.html.

STEP EIGHT

AARP. "Healthcare Costs Calculator." Accessed August 9, 2015. www.aarp.org/work
/retirement-planning/the-aarp-healthcare-costs-calculator/.

Blue Shield of California. "What Is an HSA? What Is an HSA-Compatible Health
Plan?" Accessed August 10, 2015. www.blueshieldca.com/sites/uc/non-medicare
/health-savings-plan.sp.

Edward Jones. "Healthcare and Your Retirement." Accessed August 9, 2015.
www.edwardjones.ca/groups/ejw_content/@ejw/@us/@graphics/documents
/web_content/web233376.pdf.

Fidelity. "How to Tame Retiree Healthcare Costs." June 11, 2014. Accessed August
9, 2015. www.fidelity.com/viewpoints/retirement/health-care-costs-when
-you-retire.

Forbes. "How to Get the Most Out of Your Health Savings Account." www.forbes.com
/sites/nextavenue/2013/08/27/how-to-get-the-most-out-of-your-health-savings
-account/.

Healthcare.gov. ""Health Coverage for Retirees." Accessed August 9, 2015.
www.healthcare.gov/what-if-im-retired-but-not-eligible-for-medicare/.

IRS. "Health Savings Accounts." Accessed August 9, 2015. www.irs.gov/publications
/p969/ar02.html#en_US_2014_publink1000204020.

Merrill Lynch Wealth Management. "Health and Retirement: Planning for the Great
Unknown." Accessed August 9, 2015. www.ml.com/publish/pdf/mlwm_health
-and-retirement-2014.pdf.

Index